IRON HORSES

IRON

HORSES

American Locomotives 1829-1900

E. P. ALEXANDER

BONANZA BOOKS · NEW YORK

This edition published by Bonanza Books,
a division of Crown Publishers, Inc.,
by arrangement with W. W. Norton & Company, Inc.

PRINTED IN THE UNITED STATES OF AMERICA

(B)

TO

C. L. W. *and* N. W. S.

*In Sincere Appreciation
of their Co-operation*

Contents

List of Illustrations

FIGURES

PLATES

Acknowledgments

FOR much of the assistance I have had in compiling the material for *Iron Horses* I must thank Mr. N. W. Sample, Jr. and the Franklin Institute of Philadelphia. Mr. Walter A. Lucas and Mr. Charles B. Chaney have been kind enough to supply certain data and verify much of the information contained herein. Mr. Charles L. Winey has contributed largely in furnishing many of the prints used. Several illustrations have come from the Engineering Societies Library of New York as have also three others from the Old Print Shop, also of New York. Mr. Harold Geissel has made two of the original drawings and Mr. Ward Kimball another. Other information came from Mr. Paul T. Warner of Baldwin's, Mr. Thomas T. Taber of the Railroadians, and Messrs. Charles E. Fisher and Robert R. Brown of the Railway and Locomotive Historical Society, Inc. Mr. Fisher also supplied the list of builders upon which is based that given in the back of this book.

Preface

THERE is something about a locomotive that interests and fascinates almost everyone. Perhaps it is the suggestion of latent power which it signifies, even when not in motion. Maybe its speed thrills the spectator as he watches it roar by. Or possibly, as a passenger on a train, the sensation of traveling 80 miles an hour (and more) makes him, even subconsciously, appreciative of the efficient machine "up ahead."

Modern streamline locomotives, it is often affirmed, have the most "eye appeal." But, without denying their contribution to railroading, it can safely be maintained that the picturesque engines of the last century have even more color or atmosphere. To do them justice is the purpose of this book, which is a pictorial story of their development from the first to run on rails in America to the turn of the century.

Many books have been devoted to railroads in general, but except for technical works and limited railroad historical societies' publications, little has yet been compiled to show the iron horse's growth. In a way this is not strange, since what scant information of a historical nature *is* available has been limited to that in the hands of a few collectors and specialists and is, therefore, seldom encountered by the average person. Of course, an occasional engine lithograph is infrequently unearthed by an antique or book dealer and is highly prized by its purchaser whether or not he is a railroad enthusiast. But few people actually know much about the iron horse and its changing appearance through the decades of the last century despite the almost universal interest in it.

Although many sorts of railroadiana are sought after, locomotive prints and lithographs are perhaps the most interesting to everyone. These are fast becoming extremely scarce but, aside from this consideration, what is more important is the fact that they are about the only means of portraying the early iron horses. Whether the pictorial aspect is the primary reason for the interest in them or whether the development and accomplishments of the engines they illustrated is of more importance can best be answered by the reader. Certainly the locomotives themselves should not be passed over for the artistic value of the prints. Therefore, a few original drawings showing historic engines seldom before pictured will be found among these pages.

The search for data used in this book paralleled that necessary when looking up old sailing ships. Other than prints, little information as to the exact dimensions of many of the old locomotives is to be had, because, as in the case of the shipwrights, the old engine builders considered their drawings only temporary and when their purpose had been served incontinently destroyed them. With authentic information on old motive power being scarce, that compiled and contained herein will, it is hoped, prove as interesting to the layman as to the railroad enthusiast. All data have, as far as possible, been checked and verified so that their historical accuracy is generally reliable.

The engines pictured, with the exception of some noteworthy departures from contemporary conventional design, are each typical of their respective years. Though perhaps all railroads or builders are not mentioned, the omissions do not necessarily imply that their motive power is any less interesting. Thus, if any one company or builder is more frequently represented than another, it is because perhaps better or more information on the particular engine was available. Often, the quality of the print selected has been the determining factor when deciding upon an illustration.

It should be emphasized that this volume by no means purports to be an exhaustive treatise on locomotives. Neither in its limited scope can it include mention of dozens—even hundreds—of other iron horses probably just as deserving of notice. Its purpose is rather to show a representative collection of types as locomotives evolved from the earliest primitive machines.

Iron Horses

THE story of the iron horse begins as far back as the eighteenth century when, in 1769, Nicholas Joseph Cugnot built a steam carriage which he operated on the streets of Paris. Some thirty-five years later the first American steam-propelled vehicle appeared—the *Oructor Amphibolis*. This was a crude combination carriage and boat built by Oliver Evans of Philadelphia in 1804. Nevertheless, it actually ran through the streets of that city and then made a number of trips on the Delaware. But locomotives are perhaps more correctly thought of as engines which operate on rails and are designed to pull a number of cars. According to this meaning, the first actual locomotive was built in 1803 by Richard Trevithick, a Cornishman, and is known to have hauled a load of about 9 tons. Another early locomotive was the creation of William Hedley, constructed in 1813 at Newcastle upon Tyne and named the *Puffing Billy*. Other experiments continued in England until, in 1825, George Stephenson built the *Locomotion* for the Stockton and Darlington Railway. What has been called the first really successful locomotive, however, was his *Rocket* built four years later. At a public competition, the famous Rainhill Trials, this engine won over several other entrants, among which was the *Novelty* of Braithwaite and Erics-

1. Oliver Evans's Oructor Amphibolis, *1804.*

son. This was the same Ericsson who is perhaps better known for the screw propeller and the ironclad *Monitor*.

Turning now to America, we find that, as in England, the early development of the iron horse was inextricably interwoven with that of the first railroads and their evolution depended upon each other. Although a number of short early lines were built (1809 and before) for the private transport of coal and stone, they can more accurately be called "tramways" than railroads. The first public railroad was chartered in 1815, though not built, and the incorporators of the succeeding embyro lines had, of course, horse traction in mind. Not until after 1825 were the possibilities of steam seriously considered and even then railroad builders generally were still skeptical of its practical application and of the satisfactory performance of locomotives. Regarding the subject of the kind of traction to be used, one of the earliest and perhaps least-known works (*A Treatise on Rail-Roads and Internal Communications,* Thomas Earle, Philadelphia, 1830) has this to say:

The first thing to be determined in the formation of a rail-road is the kind of power that is to be employed on it, whether horses, or steam engines. It is desirable not to use both kinds of power on the same road; because the graduation for each should be different, as will hereafter appear;—because the slow traveling of horses will present a serious obstruction to the free operations of locomotive steam engines, compelling them frequently to turn out, and occasioning delay and inconvenience; because a road for horses may be made of less strength and expensiveness than for steam carriages;

18

and because the action of the horses' feet will throw dust and gravel on the rails, which it will be desirable to avoid on roads for engines, inasmuch as it will increase the resistance, and the power required to move the wagons. A further reason is, that the dust thrown on the rails, will be converted into mud, in wet weather, and will materially diminish the adhesion of the wheels of the locomotive engine to the rails.

On the use of horses, this writer continues:

It is therefore a great desideratum to devise a mode by which a horse can perform about the same amount of work on an undulating, as he could do on a level road. This is to be effected by graduating the road in such a manner that the power expended in ascents may be returned in propelling the wagons down descents and upon levels. To effect this, the horse must *ride,* in a spare wagon, wherever the ground is descending.

Where steam is to be used, the same author gives the following advice:

It is however by no means so important for locomotive engines to preserve long continued ascents and descents. On the contrary, one composed of short undulations may be considered preferable to one of long continued ascents and descents, as the capacities of the steam engine are such, that a fund or reservoir of steam may be accumulated, while the engine and wagons are descending a declivity of moderate length by their own gravity, to enable the engine to surmount the next ascent by vigor and speed. But if descents are very long continued, the fire must be allowed to go down, or the steam to be wasted, by escaping at the safety valve.

At the same time that the first experiments with "locomotive engines" were being carried on, and the kind of power to be used was being discussed, rails were being laid. Although the question of the kind of traction was still, in most cases, a controversial subject, a notable exception to this was the decision to use steam only on the Charleston & Hamburg Railroad in South Carolina, and on this road in 1830 was operated the first steam-driven *train* in America. Generally, however, the problem waited upon satisfactory locomotives, since their efficiency was still considered doubtful compared to good horses.

One man more than any other deserves the title "Father of American Railroads." He was Colonel John Stevens of Hoboken, New Jersey, who as far back as 1811 petitioned the state legislature for a charter to permit him to construct a railroad—the first application of this sort in America. He shortly afterward reconsidered this as he decided that such an undertaking should be a public enterprise. The next year he published a pamphlet entitled "Documents Tending to Prove the Superior Advantages of Railways and Steam Carriages Over Canal Navigation" and urged Congress to consider railroad construction as a national endeavor. But the second war with England at this time claimed most attention and nothing was done. In 1815 he revived his plan of securing a charter and New Jersey granted him one to build a railway between Trenton and New Brunswick, but he could not obtain the necessary financing. In 1819 he tried to get the Pennsylvania state legislature to build a line from Philadelphia to Pittsburgh but was unsuccessful. By 1825 Stevens

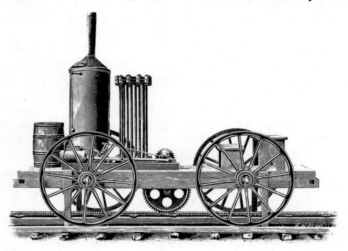

2. *John Stevens's locomotive, 1825. The upright objects in front of the boiler are its tubes set up for exhibition.*

decided to prove, at his own expense, that railroads *and locomotives* were entirely practical and built a circular railway on his Hoboken estate. By the following year he had completed a locomotive to run on the track and it made a number of trips to the astonishment of everyone who saw it. This was the first locomotive to be built and operated on rails in America. The demonstration, although not productive of immediate results, helped to give impetus to the railway movement generally.

In 1823, since he had at last abandoned the hope that the federal government could be counted upon for aid, Stevens obtained a charter in Pennsylvania for a railroad from Philadelphia to Columbia. Two prominent figures of the time—Stephen Girard and Horace Binney—aided him in this but once again, due to financial difficulties, the project

20

never got under way. This was the route adopted by the state some years later as part of the public works plan (Philadelphia & Columbia Railroad and Portage Railroad), although then Stevens had no part in it. Finally, in 1830, Colonel Stevens and his sons Robert L. and Edwin A. obtained a charter for the Camden & Amboy Railroad and Transportation Company, and, with the necessary backing secured, proceeded with this undertaking. Robert Stevens was president of the company although its affairs were jointly managed by all three. Thus at last the colonel had the satisfaction of participating in an actual railroad construction program after so many years of pioneering and disappointments.

Another of the pioneer railroaders was Horatio Allen. At the age of twenty-five, after having been engineer in charge of the construction of a section of the Delaware & Hudson Canal, he resigned in order to make a trip to England and gain a firsthand knowledge of railways. John B. Jervis, the canal company's chief engineer, made an arrangement with him to pay his expenses and commissioned him to purchase chains for the canal's inclined planes, bar-iron rails, and four locomotives for use on the levels. Accordingly he sailed in the fall of 1827 and returned the following year after having accomplished his mission. The supplies arrived about the time he did and the locomotives (three from Foster, Rastrick & Co. and one from George Stephenson) came shortly after, only the *Lion* being sent on to Honesdale (see Plate 1). The other engines were stored in New York and nothing is definitely known of their ultimate disposal. After Mr. Allen's trial trip with the *Lion* on August 8, 1829, he was appointed chief engineer of the Charleston & Hamburg Railroad. He recommended that only steam be used for traction and in January, 1830, a resolution affirming this was passed by the directors of the road. He also obtained approval for the purchase of four locomotives which were ordered from the West Point Foundry in New York, the designs being collaborated on by E. L. Miller of Charleston. The first was the *Best Friend of Charleston* which was delivered in the fall of 1830 and first tried in December of that year (see Plate 2).

While Horatio Allen was thus occupied, another man was busy with an experimental locomotive. This was Peter Cooper who was assembling his *Tom Thumb* in Baltimore. A little engine of about 1 horsepower was brought from New York and mounted on a small car frame, being geared to one axle. A tiny boiler was built, using musket barrels for

21

3. Peter Cooper's Tom Thumb *in its famous race with the horsecar, 1830.*

tubes, and a blower was devised for forcing a draught. In all, this diminutive locomotive weighed hardly more than a ton and its one cylinder was only 3½ inches in diameter with a 14-inch stroke. On August 28, 1830, drawing a boat-shaped car which carried the directors of the Baltimore & Ohio Railroad, it made its trial run, being the first locomotive in America to pull a load of passengers. Its performance was highly satisfactory despite its losing a race with a horse-drawn car on its return trip from Ellicotts Mills (due to the blower belt slipping) and Cooper definitely proved to the officials of the road the practicability of steam motive power.

The second engine to draw a train, the first having been the *Best Friend,* was also operated on the Charleston & Hamburg Railroad. It was the *West Point,* named after the firm which built it and its predecessor in New York. It was designed by E. L. Miller, this time with a horizontal boiler. Its first trip was on March 5, 1831, when it hauled four cars carrying 117 passengers a distance of 2¾ miles in 11 minutes. After the boiler of the *Best Friend* exploded, a "barrier" car loaded with cotton was advertised as a protective measure against a possible repetition of the accident.

Although not what might be called a full-sized locomotive, a miniature engine—the first built by Matthias Baldwin—is chronologically the next in line. This was built to gratify public curiosity in steam engines and Baldwin was assisted in his work by Franklin Peale, manager of the Philadelphia Museum. A track was laid around the room of this building and the little locomotive was first put into operation on April 25, 1831. It made the trip around the track many times a day for several months, drawing two small cars with seats for four persons but often pulling twice this number. Crowds came to see for the first time in Philadelphia a practical demonstration of the use of steam for railroad operation.

In January, 1831, the directors of the Baltimore & Ohio Railroad announced a public competition for the purpose of obtaining the best American locomotives. Based somewhat on the plan of the Rainhill Trials, a prize of $4,000 was offered for the best engine, entries to be ready not later than June first of that year. The *York* built by Phineas Davis of the Pennsylvania town of that name won the contest. Weighing only 3½ tons, the *York* had 30-inch drivers and an upright boiler built on the same design as Peter Cooper's. It was, as far as the records show, the only satisfactory locomotive among the five entered. One was built by Ezekiel Childs of Philadelphia, a watchmaker—as were also Baldwin and Davis. This used a rotary steam engine which in a model had promised good results. It was designed to produce 50 horsepower but did not prove practical. Another was Stacey Costell's engine which had four connected 36-inch driving wheels. Two 6-inch cylinders of 12-inch stroke had their pistons connected to cranks on a countershaft which in turn was geared to one of the axles. Nothing much is known of this machine and it is even doubtful whether it was actually sent from Philadelphia to Baltimore. George W. Johnson of Baltimore, in whose shop the *Tom Thumb* had been assembled, was the builder of the fourth entry. This, as were all the others, was a four-wheeled engine, two of which were drivers. Two vertical cylinders were used which transmitted power to the wheels through walking beams mounted on top of the firebox. The last entrant was William T. James of New York (though

4. The West Point *of the Charleston & Hamburg Railroad, 1831.*

23

the date is sometimes given as 1832), who entered his sixth engine, others having been experiments and models. The boiler was upright and the cylinders, set at a 30-degree angle, were 10 by 10 inches. Power was transmitted through a shaft and an elementary form of gearshift, the forerunner of that used in automobiles. The peculiar boiler construction with inward projecting tubes was weak and it soon exploded.

5. James's entrant in the Baltimore & Ohio contest, 1831.

Although the *DeWitt Clinton* is generally given credit for being the third engine to haul a train in America, according to available dates one other actually preceded it. This was an unnamed engine, designed by Colonel Stephen Long for the New Castle and Frenchtown Railroad, which made its trial trip on July 4, 1831. It was not, however, too successful, although it hauled two cars with about seventy people, as it was incapable of furnishing sufficient steam and was later rebuilt.

Next came the well-known *DeWitt Clinton*, built for the Mohawk and Hudson Railroad by the West Point Foundry. Designed by John B. Jervis, its total weight with tender was 12,098 pounds. It made a trial run in July, 1831, and on August 9 made the 17-mile trip from Albany to Schenectady in less than an hour. Its wheels were 54 inches in diameter and all were drivers. The lower part of the tender was actually a tank for the water supply, probably the first "water-bottom tank" ever used. Its train usually consisted of stagecoach-type cars. It was not particularly successful and was broken up a few years later. The replica frequently seen was built in 1892 for the Columbian Exposition.

Since we are tracing this early motive-power history by dates of first operation rather than when the various locomotives were built, the next we find is the famous *John Bull*, which was actually being constructed in England about the time that Baldwin was building his first model. After the Camden & Amboy Railroad was chartered, Robert Stevens, who was chief engineer as well as president, went to England in October of 1830. His mission was to purchase rails and other track equipment as well as a locomotive. He was familiar with the types of rails then in use and, to pass the time on shipboard, designed and whittled several models of improved rail section—the first H rail ever devised (commonly called T rail today). He also designed the hook-headed spike for fastening it. Upon his arrival in England, Francis B. Ogden, the United States Consul at Liverpool, introduced him to John Guest whose firm in Dowlais, Wales, was persuaded to undertake the rolling of the new rail. There was at first some difficulty in straightening it as it came from

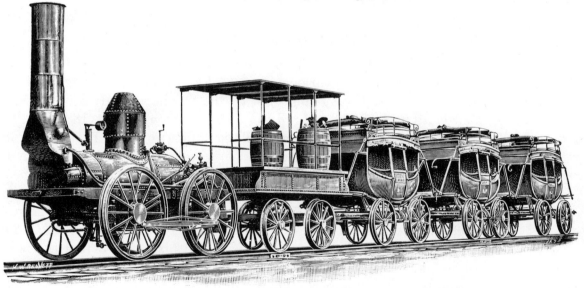

6. *The* DeWitt Clinton *of the Mohawk and Hudson Railroad, 1831.*

the rolls but this was soon remedied. The lengths supplied were 12, 15, and 18 feet, the weight of that first produced being 36 pounds to the yard and that made later 42 pounds per yard.

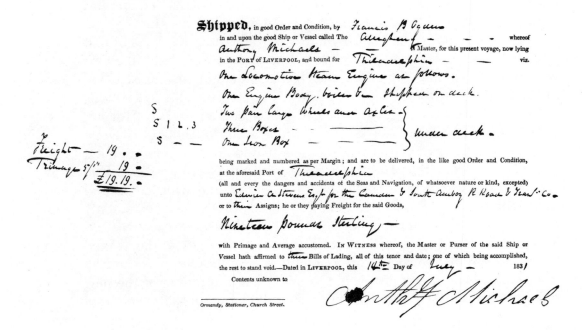

7. Bill of lading for the John Bull, *1831.*

While the necessary rail and fastenings were being manufactured, the locomotive known variously as *John Bull,* Number 1, or *Stevens* had been ordered and was being built by the Stephensons. It was shipped shortly after the first lot of rail from Liverpool on July 14, 1831, by the packet *Allegheny* and arrived at Philadelphia in June. From there it was sent to Bordentown where the parts were assembled and where it was first tried in November, 1831, going into regular passenger service two years later. It is interesting to note that while it remained at Bordentown Matthias Baldwin inspected it, and his first full-sized engine reflected some of its features of construction. Figure 8 shows the *John Bull* as it appeared when rebuilt with the first pilot or cowcatcher, while Plate 3 shows it as first assembled.

Another English importation, the *Robert Fulton,* received by the Mohawk and Hudson Road at about the same time as the *John Bull* arrived,

26

should be mentioned. It was generally similar in design, being of the so-called Samson class, but not so successful. Still another locomotive built abroad was the *Herald* for the Baltimore and Susquehanna Railroad. This line had 7 miles of track ready in 1831 but the exact date when this engine was received and run is not recorded.

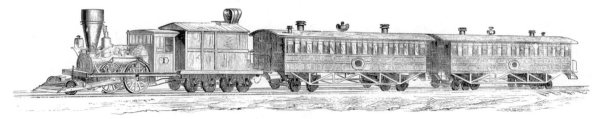

8. *The* John Bull *as rebuilt about 1833. The cab was a still later addition.*

In 1832 at least six locomotives were added to the growing stud of iron horses. One was the *Brother Jonathan*, also known as the *Experiment*, designed by John B. Jervis and built by the West Point Foundry. It was notable in that it was the first to use a leading or engine truck (although Ross Winans installed one on the *Herald* about this time) and was built for the Mohawk and Hudson Railroad. It was the world's

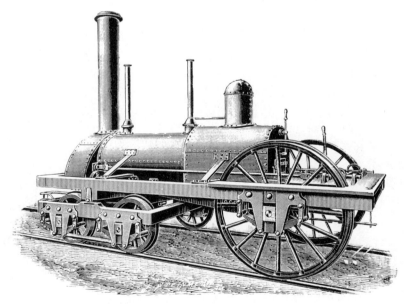

9. *The* Brother Jonathan, *1832.*

27

fastest locomotive in its day, speeds of as much as 60 miles an hour being attributed to it. It had cylinders 9½ by 16 inches and its drivers were 60 inches in diameter.

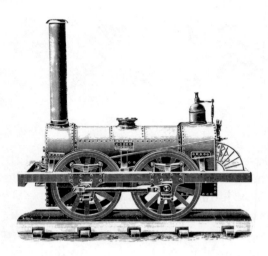

10. The Herald *of the Baltimore and Susquehanna Railroad, 1832.*

Another engine by the same builder was the *South Carolina* designed by Horatio Allen for the Charleston & Hamburg Road, the first eight-wheeled locomotive in America. It had a double-ended boiler with the firebox in the middle, the firedoor being on the side, and flexible piping to the cylinders.

Matthias Baldwin enters the picture here with his first full-sized engine, the first successful one built in Pennsylvania and the forerunner of the long line of locomotives which made his name almost synonymous with the industry. It was built for the Philadelphia, Germantown and Norristown Road and was of the design known as the Planet type. It was far superior to any of the imported engines then in service, though at first a few defects had to be corrected. It developed a speed of 30 miles an hour and was used for over twenty years.

The second engine built by Phineas Davis (the firm name being Davis and Gartner) was the *Atlantic,* today the second oldest locomotive in

11. *The* South Carolina *of the Charleston & Hamburg Railroad, 1832.*

existence in America and still maintained in working order. It was the first of the so-called "grasshopper" type and was a considerable improvement over the *York,* having also been built for the Baltimore & Ohio. All of its wheels were drivers, but its 6½-ton weight, two 10 by 20-inch cylinders, and an efficient boiler enabled it to haul 30 tons at a speed of 15 miles an hour. Its cost of operation, based principally on the comparatively small amount of coal consumed, was less than half that of proportionate horsepower.

One more engine as well as the road it operated on must be mentioned for 1832. This was the *Pontchartrain* of the railroad of the same name which connected New Orleans and Lake Pontchartrain. Though the latter was joined to the city by a canal, the time for the trip took so long that a speedier method was desired and this resulted in the railroad's being chartered in 1830. The same American consul, Francis Ogden, with whom Robert Stevens had had dealings, helped with the purchasing of the rails in England and the road was formally opened with

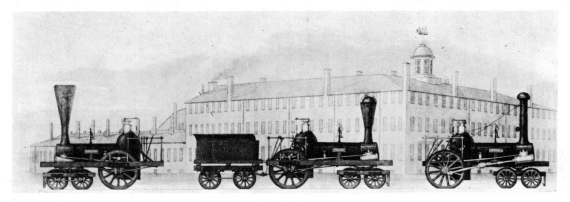

12. *The Baldwin Locomotive Works and three of its products as pictured in a lithograph of the eighteen thirties.*

29

horsepower on April 23, 1831. In June, 1832, a locomotive built by John Shields of Cincinnati was tried but was unsuccessful. The *Pontchartrain* was then ordered from England and on September 17, 1832, made its first regular run.

From 1832 on, the roster of locomotives increased so rapidly that individual mention is impossible and the tracing of more than a few of the more outstanding engines is beyond the scope of this brief sketch. Thus, for instance, Baldwin's second engine should be mentioned. This was the *E. L. Miller,* ordered in 1833 and delivered to the South Carolina Road (previously called the Charleston & Hamburg) in March, 1834. It was named after the same Mr. Miller who was responsible for several of the road's earliest motive power and he collaborated with Baldwin on the engine's design. This type of engine became practically standard with the Baldwin Works for several years and its appearance was similar to that of the *Lancaster* (Figure 13).

When the state of Pennsylvania finally authorized the construction of the Philadelphia & Columbia Railroad, a distance of 82 miles, the line was so surveyed that the maximum grade was 30 feet to the mile. At each end was an inclined plane where stationary engines hauled the trains up the long grades. The plane at the Philadelphia end was 2,805 feet long with a rise of 377 feet to the mile and was known as the Belmont Incline. That at the Columbia end was 1,800 feet long and had a grade of 264 feet to the mile. Stationary engines were used to draw brigades of cars up these inclines until, in 1836, Norris's *George Washington* (Plate 7) proved itself capable of surmounting such a grade.

The road was opened officially on April 16, 1834, and for ten years, until locomotives became the exclusive motive power, all sorts of horse-drawn vehicles, both public and private, were used as well as locomotives. In June, 1834, Baldwin delivered the *Lancaster,* his third engine

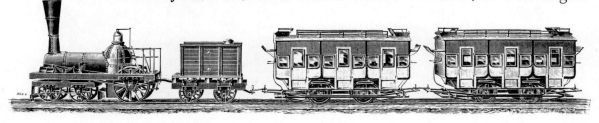

13. Baldwin's Lancaster *of the Philadelphia & Columbia Railroad, 1834.*

(Figure 13), which proved very successful. This was followed by his fourth, the *Columbia*, in September and another engine in November. All these engines had 54-inch driving wheels, 9 by 16-inch cylinders, and weighed about 17,000 pounds.

A traveler journeying from Philadelphia to Pittsburgh after 1834 would use this road to Columbia, a distance of 82 miles. Here he would change to a canalboat traversing the state's system for 180 miles to Hollidaysburg. From Hollidaysburg to Johnstown he would take passage over the Portage Road, a railroad over the crest of the Allegheny Mountains 36 miles in length. This road used stationary engines to handle the cars over ten inclined planes, the highest point being 1,339 feet above sea level, although locomotives and horses were used for the eleven levels. The descent to Johnstown was 1,171 feet, and at that point he would again board a canalboat for the remainder of his journey to Pittsburgh.

Charles Dickens in his *American Notes* says of his trip over this road in 1842:

On Sunday morning we arrived at the foot of the mountain, which is crossed by railroad. There are ten inclined planes; five ascending, and five descending; the carriages are dragged up the former, and let slowly down the latter, by means of stationary engines; the comparatively level spaces between, being traversed, sometimes by horse, and sometimes by engine power, as the case demands. Occasionally the rails are laid upon the extreme verge of a giddy precipice; and, looking from the carriage window, the traveler gazes sheer down, without a stone or scrap of fence between, into the mountain depths below. The journey is very carefully made, however; only two carriages traveling together; and while proper precautions are taken, is not to be dreaded for its dangers.

It was very pretty, traveling thus at a rapid pace along the heights of the mountain in a keen wind, to look down into a valley full of light and softness; catching glimpses, through the tree-tops, of scattered cabins; children running to the doors, dogs bursting out to bark, whom we could see without hearing; terrified pigs scampering homeward; families sitting out in their rude gardens; cows gazing upward with a stupid indifference; men in their shirt-sleeves looking on at their unfinished houses, planning tomorrow's work; and we riding onward, high above them, like a whirlwind. It was amusing, too, when we had dived, and rattled down a steep pass, having no other moving power than the weight of the carriages themselves, to see the engine released, long after us, come buzzing down alone, like a great insect, its back of green and gold so shining in the sun, that if it had spread a pair of wings and soared away, no one would have had occasion, as I fancied, for the least surprise.

31

14. Campbell's 4–4–0 engine for the Philadelphia, Germantown, and Norristown Railroad, 1836.

But it stopped short of us in a very business-like manner when we reached the canal: and, before we left the wharf, went panting up this hill again, with the passengers who had waited our arrival for the means of traversing the road by which we had come.

In 1836 the first 4–4–0 or American-type locomotive was patented by Henry R. Campbell "in order to distribute the weight of the engine upon the rails more completely," with the axles of the driving wheels in front of and behind the firebox. The first engine of this type was built by James Brooks of Philadelphia for the Philadelphia, Germantown and Norristown Road and, though not too successful, was a definite step forward. Its principal defect was in not having a method of equalizing the weight on the drivers. This was done on the next engine of this wheel arrangement built by Garrett & Eastwick for the Beaver Meadow Railroad (Plate 8).

In 1836 the *Pioneer*, Baldwin's thirty-seventh locomotive, was built for the Utica & Schenectady Railroad. After some years of service it was sold to the Michigan Central Railroad where it was called the *Alert* and some improvements were made. In 1848 it again changed hands, going to the Galena & Chicago Union Railroad, now part of the Chicago &

Northwestern Railway, and was renamed the *Pioneer*.

Thomas Rogers's first locomotive, the *Sandusky*, was completed in 1837 and, though built for the New Jersey Railroad and Transportation Company, was acquired by the Mad River & Lake Erie Railroad. No tracks had yet been laid when the engine reached Sandusky by boat and the new line was built to conform to its gauge—4 feet 10 inches. The Ohio state legislature, as a result, enacted a law making its gauge standard for all railroads to be built in Ohio. The *Sandusky's* cylinders were 11 by 16 inches and its driving wheels with cast-iron centers and hollow spokes were among the first to have counterbalances.

Following the "grasshopper" engines on the Baltimore & Ohio, another odd design introduced in 1837 should be noted. These were the locomotives known as "crabs," so named because they seemed to run backward. In this type, developed by Ross Winans, the boiler still remained upright (as in the previous design) but the cylinders were placed horizontally. The drivers were 36 inches in diameter, the cylinders 12½ by 24 inches, and the total weight was 12 tons.

One section of the country perhaps a little late in getting started with railroad construction, but making up for it later in extensive building, was New England. The first three roads to be chartered there were

15. Thomas Rogers's first locomotive, the Sandusky, *1837.*

16. One of the first "crab" type locomotives on the Baltimore & Ohio Railroad.

the Boston & Lowell in 1830, and the Boston & Providence and Boston & Worcester in 1831. Though all three used horsepower at first, the Boston *Advertiser* of March 24, 1834, had this announcement regarding the Boston & Worcester:

The rails are laid from Boston to Newton, a distance of nine or ten miles, to which place it is proposed to run the passenger cars as soon as two loco-motives shall be in readiness, so as to insure regularity. One locomotive, called the "Meteor," has been partially tried and will probably be in readiness in a few days; the second, called the "Rocket," is waiting the arrival of the builder for subjecting it to a trial, and the third, it is hoped, will be ready by the first of May.

According to advertisements in the newspapers, regular passenger service was established between Boston and Newton on May 16, 1834, and later in the same year extensions of the road were opened to Hopkinton and Westboro.

One of the last of the pioneer railroad enterprises to get started was the New York & Erie Railroad. The people of New York had the Erie Canal, with excellent facilities for water-borne traffic, and were consequently very apathetic toward railroad construction compared with that then planned and under way in Maryland, Pennsylvania, South

34

Carolina, and New England. However, in 1833, after a long series of meetings which accomplished little but delay, the Erie was finally organized. More delays and difficulties, largely financial, postponed any actual construction until 1835. The line's terminus was at Piermont, about 25 miles from New York, but grading was commenced far inland as well. Much of the work was useless, such as long stretches of piling which were never used. Such needless expense caused continual financial difficulties so that not until 1841 was a short section to Ramapo and a little later to Goshen opened for business, the broad gauge of 6 feet having been decided on. For motive power, George H. Hoffman, the chief engineer, had ordered three engines from William Norris of Philadelphia in 1840, these to be partly paid for in Erie stock and to cost $8,000 each. The first was the *Eleazer Lord,* named after the president of the road; the second was the *Piermont;* and the third was the *Rockland.* All were American-type or 4–4–0 engines and their average weight was 32,000 pounds. The cylinders were 13 by 20 inches and, like other engines of this period, none had cabs.

17. The first "Mud Digger" type designed by Ross Winans and built by M. W. Baldwin for the Western Railroad of Massachusetts, 1844.

35

Early in 1841 Numbers 4 and 5, the *Orange* and *Ramapo,* were received, also having been built by Norris. The former weighed 30,700 pounds with 21,100 pounds on the 55-inch driving wheels and had 10¾ by 18-inch cylinders. The *Orange* was probably the Erie's most famous early locomotive, having been run on a number of special occasions. One was in 1842 when it helped bring a message from Governor Seward to the New York *Sun* in time to "scoop" its rival, the *Herald.* The latter believed that the stage line across the Hudson was faster and the race was arranged. Both couriers left Albany at the same time, one bringing the message to Goshen where the *Orange* was waiting to bring it to Piermont. The *Sun* had typesetters waiting on the steamship and the paper was composed and ready to go to press by the time it reached New York, thus getting on the street an hour before the *Herald's* rider arrived. The *Orange* was also first at other events, such as openings of new extensions of the line, but after having been sold to two other roads in turn it disappeared, the last known reference to her by date being in 1853. Numbers 6 and 7 of the Erie's motive power were the *Sussex* and *Sullivan,* both Rogers engines. Baldwin built Numbers 8 and 9, the *New York* and *Monroe.*

In 1849, the same year that the *John Stevens* (Plate 21) was first run, another engine with large driving wheels was delivered by Edward Norris to the Utica and Schenectady Railroad. This was the *Lightning,* whose single pair of drivers was 84 inches in diameter. The cylinders were 16 by 22 inches and the boiler diameter was 42 inches, the weight being 20 tons. This engine was unusual in that the load on the drivers could be changed by varying a fulcrum pin between the equalizer and the frame. All wheels were solid forgings, the first of their kind in America. The engine was very fast, having been known to have hauled eight 8-wheeled cars a distance of 16 miles in 13 minutes, but it was in service little more than a year.

Such were most of the first and a few of the later pioneer locomotives in America. A few others might have been mentioned but their history is so obscured by time that, except for their names, they have been almost forgotten. Since these early days the gradual evolution of the iron horse is evidenced by the succeeding plates and short descriptions. But even these, though representing nearly every year until 1900, cannot do more than present in brief the locomotive's share in railroading. It

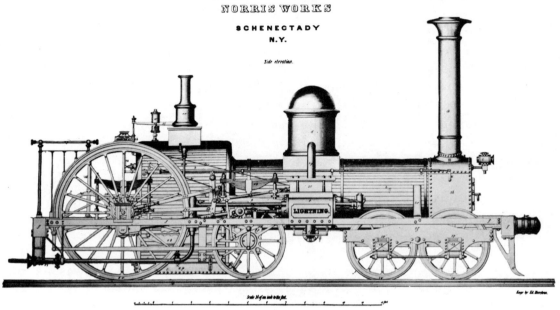

EXPRESS-PASSENGER-ENGINE

"LIGHTNING"

BUILT BY E.S. NORRIS

NORRIS WORKS

SCHENECTADY
N.Y.

Side elevation.

18. The Lightning *of the Utica and Schenectady Railroad, 1849.*

is obvious, of course, that as this machine grew and became increasingly capable and powerful its consequent effect on railroad expansion became more pronounced. But it is not so much the economic or technical aspect which is considered in the following pages, nor is there much of railroad history. Rather, the illustrations and case histories or sketches are intended to furnish a graphic story of railroad lore which is as much a contribution to Americana in general as any other development of science, engineering, or the arts.

PLATES

ORDERED by Horatio Allen for the Delaware & Hudson Canal Company from the firm of Foster, Rastrick & Company of Stourbridge, England, this was the first actual locomotive (as distinguished from experimental engines) to run in America. It was shipped from Liverpool on April 8 and arrived in New York on May 15, having actually been built before the famous *Rocket* of Stephenson. It was sent by river boat to Roundout and then by canal to Honesdale, arriving there on July 23. On August 8, 1829, it made its trial trip, being operated by Horatio Allen.

It was intended that this and the other locomotives which were never run (page 21) be used for hauling coal from Carbondale to Honesdale. The track crossed the Lackawaxen Creek on a trestle but it was considered unsafe for the engine, which was found to weigh more than twice as much as the 3 tons specified in the contract. But steam having been raised, despite the efforts of friends to dissuade him, Allen alone ran the *Lion* back and forth across the trestle, at about 10 miles an hour.

Though the *Lion* proved itself capable, it was not used again and was stored near by. Eventually it was broken up, but some parts were located and are now in the National Museum in Washington.

The *Lion* cost $3,000. It weighed 7 tons and had vertical cylinders, all wheels being coupled. The wheels were of oak with iron tires and "grasshopper" beams were used to transmit the power to them from the cylinders. Most accounts say a painting of a lion's head appeared on its boiler front.

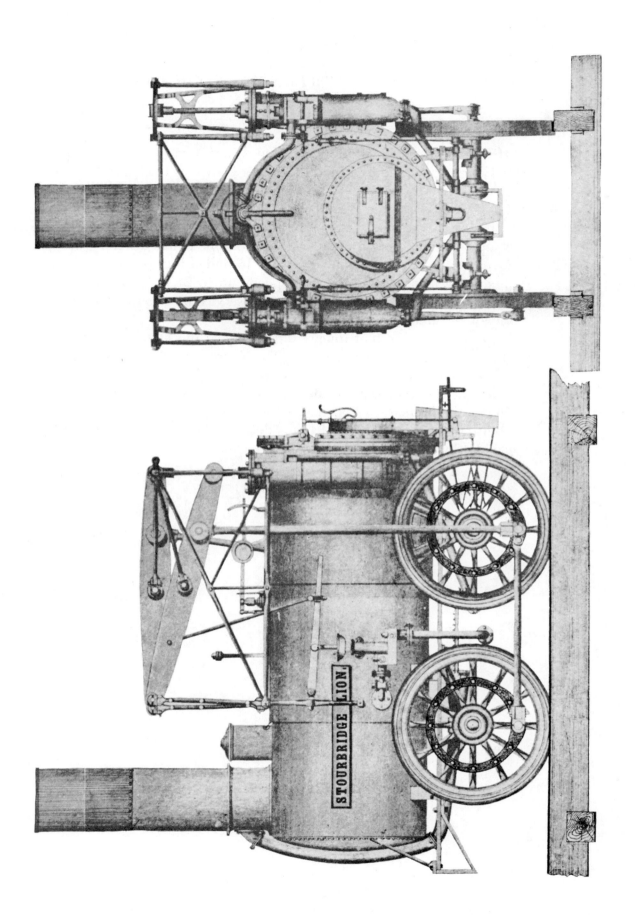

THE first locomotive to draw a train in America was contracted for by the Charleston & Hamburg Railroad, later known as the South Carolina Railroad. It was designed by E. L. Miller of Charleston and ordered in March, 1830, from the West Point Foundry of New York. In October of that year it was sent by ocean packet to Charleston, where it was set up by Julius Petsch and Nicholas Darrell. It had its trial run on November 2 and on December 14 and 15 pulled four or five cars with some forty to fifty passengers at speeds up to 21 miles an hour. On January 15, 1831, it inaugurated regular service on this railroad with a brigade of three cars.

On the seventeenth of June of the same year this engine was the first on record to have a boiler explosion. The Negro fireman became annoyed with the sound of escaping steam from the safety valve and held down its lever. The explosion scalded the engineer, Nicholas Darrell, and injured the fireman so that he died a few days later. The engine was rebuilt under the direction of Julius Petsch, who was appointed master machinist of the road, and renamed *Phoenix*.

Cylinders 6 by 16 inches   Weight 4½ tons   Driving wheel 54 inches in diameter
Steam pressure 50 pounds   Tractive effort 400 pounds

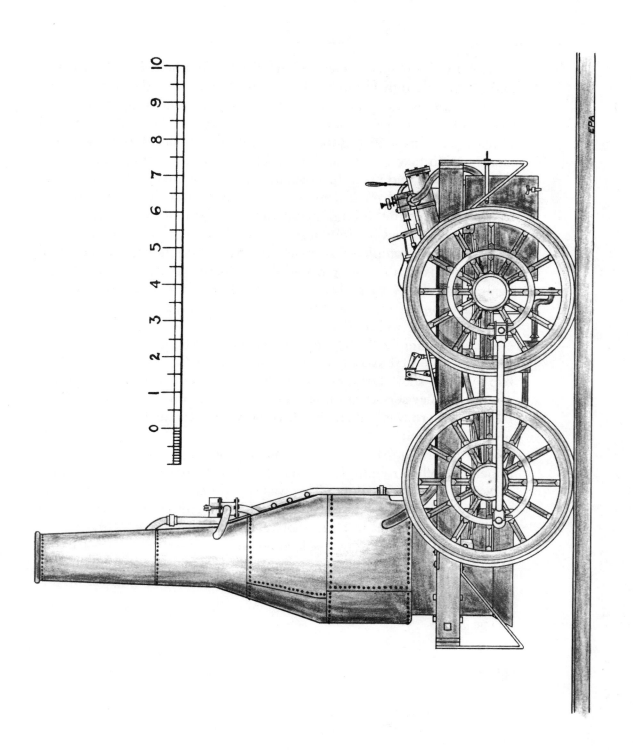

BUILT by the works of George and Robert Stephenson at Newcastle upon Tyne, though familiarly known by the above title, it is perhaps more accurately designated as Number 1 of the Camden & Amboy Railroad, being also occasionally called the *Stevens*. After its arrival in Philadelphia (page 25), Robert Stevens engaged Isaac Dripps, a young mechanic, to take charge and assemble the engine. Dripps had it put aboard a sloop and taken to Bordentown and then hauled by wagon to a ¾-mile length of track near the town. Here, in a shed adjoining the track, Dripps put the engine together. He had never before seen a locomotive and had no drawings or other dimensions to guide him, but he successfully completed its assembly. Since no tender had been supplied, Dripps made a four-wheeled car, to the platform of which he fastened a whisky cask obtained from a Bordentown grocery. A local shoemaker made him a leather pipe for the water-supply connection between engine and tender.

On November 12, 1831, the members of the New Jersey state legislature were the first passengers to be hauled by this engine on its trial trip over the short section of track then laid down. The engine did not go into regular service until late in 1833 when other engines had been built and there was sufficient motive power as well as trackage to commence operation.

The illustration shows the locomotive approximately as it originally appeared. When rebuilt, the connecting rods were removed and a pilot, designed by Dripps, added. This was found necessary both to push obstructions off the track and to help guide the engine on curves. It was the first ever applied to a locomotive (see Figure 8 page 27).

The *John Bull* is the oldest locomotive preserved in America today. It has made a number of trips, notably to the Columbian Exposition in 1893, under its own steam. It is now preserved in the National Museum.

Cylinders 9 by 20 inches   Weight 10 tons   Drivers 54 inches in diameter Gauge 5 feet

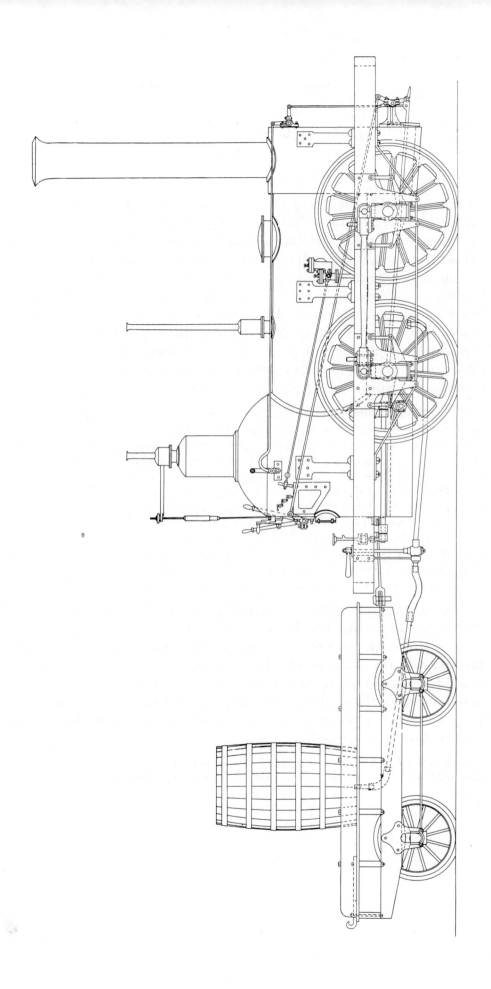

4

AS A result of the success of his model locomotive at the Philadelphia Museum in 1831, Matthias Baldwin was given an order for a locomotive to be used on the Philadelphia, Germantown and Norristown Railroad, a short line 6 miles in length then operated with horses. In building this engine, which he named *Old Ironsides,* Baldwin had considerable difficulties to surmount as there were few competent mechanics and fewer suitable tools. Much of the work later done by machines was then necessarily entirely done by hand. Nevertheless, the engine was finally completed and, though some improvements were found necessary, was put into regular service three days after its trial on November 23, 1832. The *Chronicle* of November 24 of that year says:

It gives us pleasure to state that the locomotive engine built by our townsman, M. W. Baldwin, has proved highly successful. In the presence of several gentlemen of science and information on such subjects, the engine was yesterday placed upon the road for the first time. All her parts had been previously highly finished and fitted together in Mr. Baldwin's factory. . . . The placing fire in the furnace and raising steam occupied 20 minutes. The engine (with her tender) moved from the depot in beautiful style, working with great ease and uniformity. She proceeded about half a mile beyond the Union Tavern, at the township line, and returned immediately, a distance of six miles, at a speed of about 28 miles to the hour, her speed having been slackened at all the road crossings, and it being after dark, but a portion of her power was used. It is needless to say that the spectators were delighted.

The agreed price of the engine had been $4,000, but because of the defects already mentioned Baldwin had some difficulty in securing his money. However, after the necessary changes had been made, a compromise was reached whereby the amount paid was $3,500. Baldwin was discouraged because of the difficulties encountered and the trouble in obtaining a settlement and told a friend "That is our last locomotive." But only about a year was to elapse before he was to undertake the construction of his second.

Cylinders 9½ by 18 inches   Weight 11,000 pounds   Drivers 54 inches in diameter Boiler 30 inches in diameter   Front wheels 45 inches in diameter

46

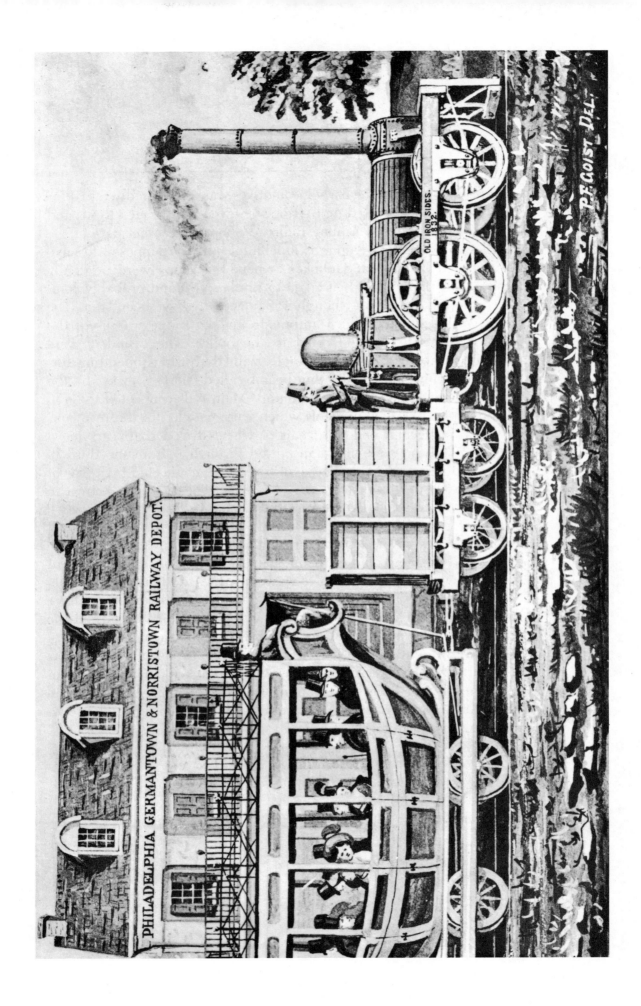

ONE of the oddest of the early locomotives was undoubtedly the *Monster,* a design collaborated on by Robert Stevens and Isaac Dripps and built by the Camden & Amboy Railroad Shops. The exact date of the completion of the first engine is indefinite, but it is supposed to have been started in 1833 at Hoboken, where the shops were originally located. The parts were then taken to Bordentown and probably completed the following year, though it may actually have been later. The boiler was designed to burn anthracite and no frame was used, the axle-box pedestals being riveted to the boiler. The cylinders were mounted at about a 30-degree angle, with the pistons operating forward and connected to vibrating beams called "horse's necks" by the men, and which moved like pendulums. Main rods connected these to the third pair of driving wheels which were coupled to the rear pair. Between the second and third pair of wheels was a shaft carrying a spur gear, the power being transmitted through it from the third to the second pair of drivers. These, in turn, were connected by a pair of coupling rods to the leading pair of wheels. The gear was known to have broken occasionally, causing the engine to lose half its tractive power.

The first boiler was not too satisfactory, and after having been in service awhile blew off the steam dome. Mr. Dripps, then "Chief of Motive Power" (the first man to bear this title) designed a new one.

The boiler was rebuilt and improved upon so that its steaming qualities were increased. The engine was sufficiently satisfactory to warrant the ordering of three more Monsters from the Trenton Locomotive Works, which were founded in 1853, Mr. Dripps being one of the partners of the firm. At least one Monster was rebuilt as a 4–6–0 in 1869, becoming Pennsylvania Railroad's Number 635, and was in service several years. As Sinclair puts it, ". . . a strange-looking Monster to be prowling about on our railroads at as late a day as 1875."

Cylinders 18 by 30 inches   Weight 60,900 pounds   Drivers 48 inches in diameter

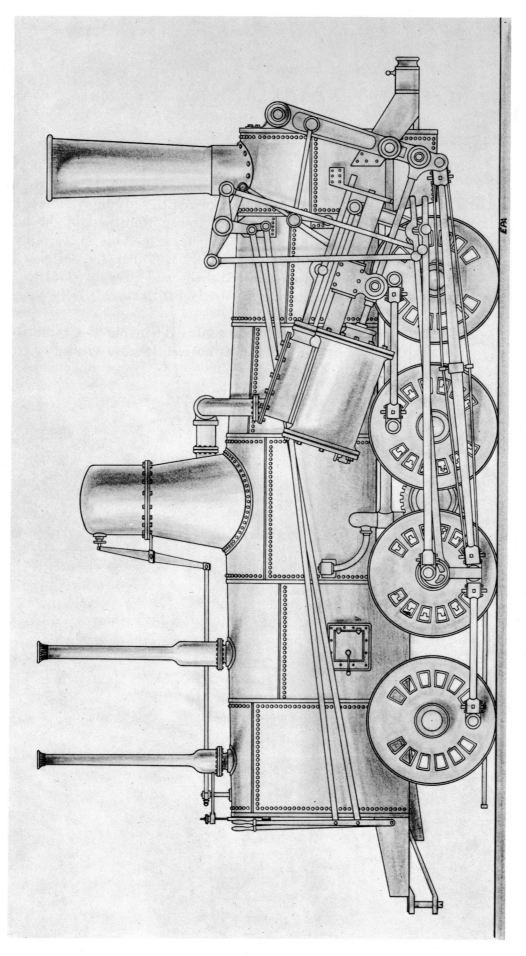

BALDWIN'S eleventh locomotive was completed in May, 1835, and delivered to the Philadelphia & Trenton Railroad. Named the *Black Hawk,* it was the first Baldwin engine with outside cylinders. It was also the first to use the method of transmitting part of the tender's weight to the locomotive in order to increase traction. This arrangement had been patented in June, 1831, by E. L. Miller, the designer of the South Carolina Road's engines. Baldwin paid a royalty of $100 on this and other engines on which it was used until, in May, 1839, he purchased the patent rights for $9,000.

This *Black Hawk* should not be confused with another, built by Long & Norris a little earlier, which was not nearly as successful.

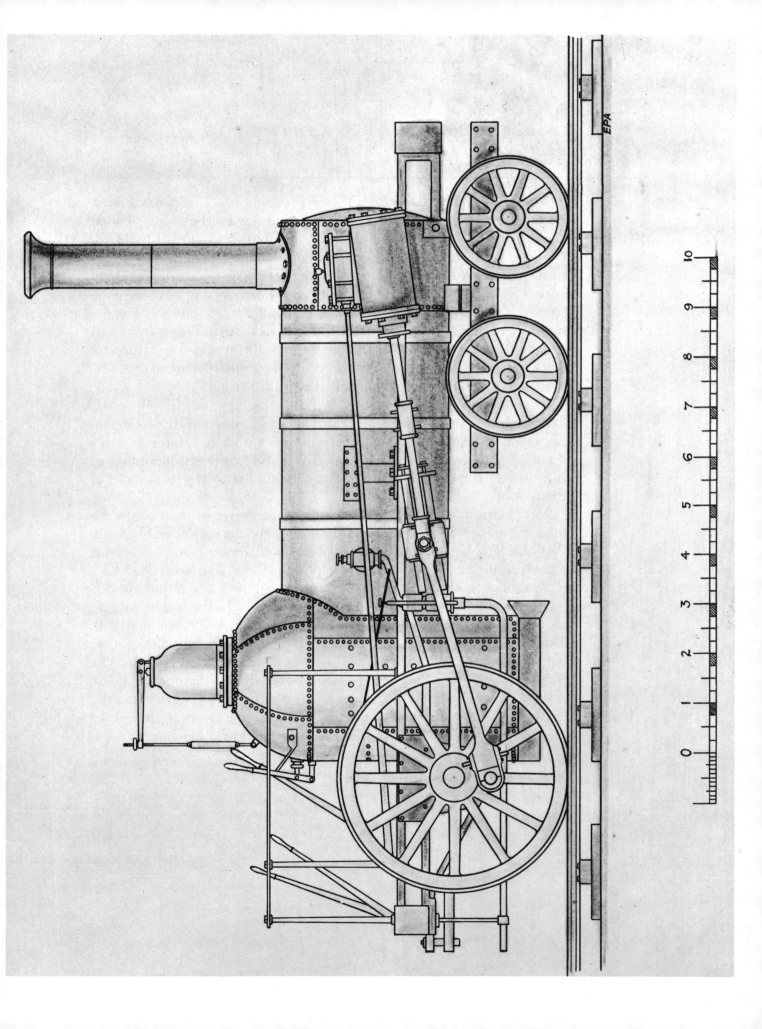

7   *1836. THE GEORGE WASHINGTON*

ON JULY 10, 1836, the *George Washington*, built by William Norris of Philadelphia, hauled a load of 19,200 pounds up the Belmont inclined plane at the Philadelphia end of the Philadelphia & Columbia Railroad. This was regarded as a most unusual and remarkable achievement because previously no engine had ever attempted such a feat, the cars having been pulled up the grade by cables and stationary engines (see page 30). Not only did this engine climb a grade of 1 in 14, but it attained a speed of 15 miles an hour while working under a steam pressure of but 60 pounds. So successful was the test that the Birmingham & Gloucester Railway in England gave Norris an order for similar locomotives to be used on the Lickey Incline, which had a grade of 1 in 37.

It is not known definitely whether this engine was "inside connected" (meaning that the cylinders were inside the frames, with the rods connected to cranked axles) or as shown, and authorities differ as to its exact appearance. The illustration cannot be positively identified as being exactly correct, but it is reasonably similar to Norris engines of that period.

A comparison with the early Baldwin single-driver engines is very interesting since it shows the similarity of thought among the first locomotive builders. Up to 1842 Baldwin furnished some 27 engines of this wheel arrangement to the Philadelphia & Columbia Road and they were similar in most respects to the Norris engines. The important difference was in the position of the driving wheels. In the Norris engines they were in front of the firebox while Baldwin placed them behind it. Thus the former, carrying a greater portion of their weight on the driving wheels, had more adhesion with consequent increased traction. The Baldwin engines, on the contrary, while not having the hauling capacity, were the more steady riders. The result was that they were generally used for passenger service while the Norris engines were preferred for freight (see Plate 6 for comparison with the Baldwin machine).

Cylinders 10¼ by 17⅝ inches   Total weight 14,930 pounds   Drivers 48 inches in diameter   Weight on drivers 8,700 pounds

52

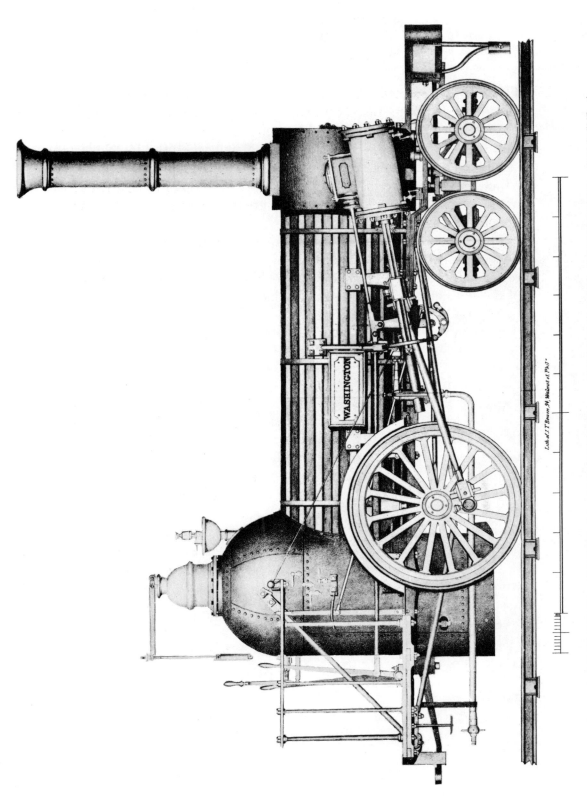

LOCOMOTIVE STEAM ENGINE of WILLIAM NORRIS, PHILa.

CLASS B.

Lith. of J.T. Bowen, 94. Walnut st. Phila

WASHINGTON

THE firm of Garrett & Eastwick of Philadelphia had already built one locomotive for the Beaver Meadow Railroad (called the *Samuel D. Ingham* after its president) and had engaged as foreman Joseph Harrison, Jr., who had worked with William Norris when the *Hercules,* their second engine for this road, was ordered late in 1836. It was the first on which a type of driving wheel equalizer, developed by Harrison, was used. This locomotive proved to be a great success and led to other orders for the same class of engines.

The *Hercules* had a separate frame with pedestals or supports in which the driving wheel axles were placed. The weight of the engine rested upon the center of this frame, thus allowing better adjustment of the wheels to uneven track than the rigid frames previously used.

Weight 15 tons

THE *Essex* was built for the Morris & Essex Railroad in 1838 by Seth Boyden of Newark, New Jersey, being completed in May. It was used in active service until 1851 when it was sold to the Iron Railroad Company of Ohio. It is now somewhere on the bottom of Lake Erie as the schooner upon which it was being transported to its new owners foundered in a storm.

Although no authentic records are available, it is probable that the dimensions of the *Essex* were about the same as those of its predecessor, the *Orange,* which was built by Boyden in 1837. These were Boyden's first two locomotives.

Cylinders 8½ by 26 inches   Weight 6 tons   Driving wheels 53½ inches in diameter

IN THE summer of 1839 Eastwick & Harrison (the latter having been made a partner) received an order from the Philadelphia & Reading Railway for a freight engine. The road's chief engineer, Moncure Robinson, specified an engine which was to burn anthracite coal in a horizontal, tubular boiler. It was not to weigh more than 11 tons, 9 of which were to rest on the drivers. The *Gowan & Marx* was designed on the plan of the *Hercules* and, to distribute its weight, the rear axle was placed under the firebox. A blower of the steam-jet type was used for the first time on this engine.

When put into service, the *Gowan & Marx* proved to be extraordinarily powerful. On one of its trips (February 20, 1840) it hauled a train of 101 loaded four-wheeled cars from Reading to Philadelphia at an average speed of 9.82 miles an hour. The train's gross load was 423 tons and, if the weight of the engine and tender is included, the total was forty times the engine's weight. This was believed to excel any performance on record for an 11-ton locomotive. Its great success led the Philadelphia & Reading to duplicate its design in ten engines later built for them at Lowell, Mass.

Cylinders 12⅛ by 18 inches Weight 11 tons Driving wheels 42 inches in diameter Weight on drivers 9 tons

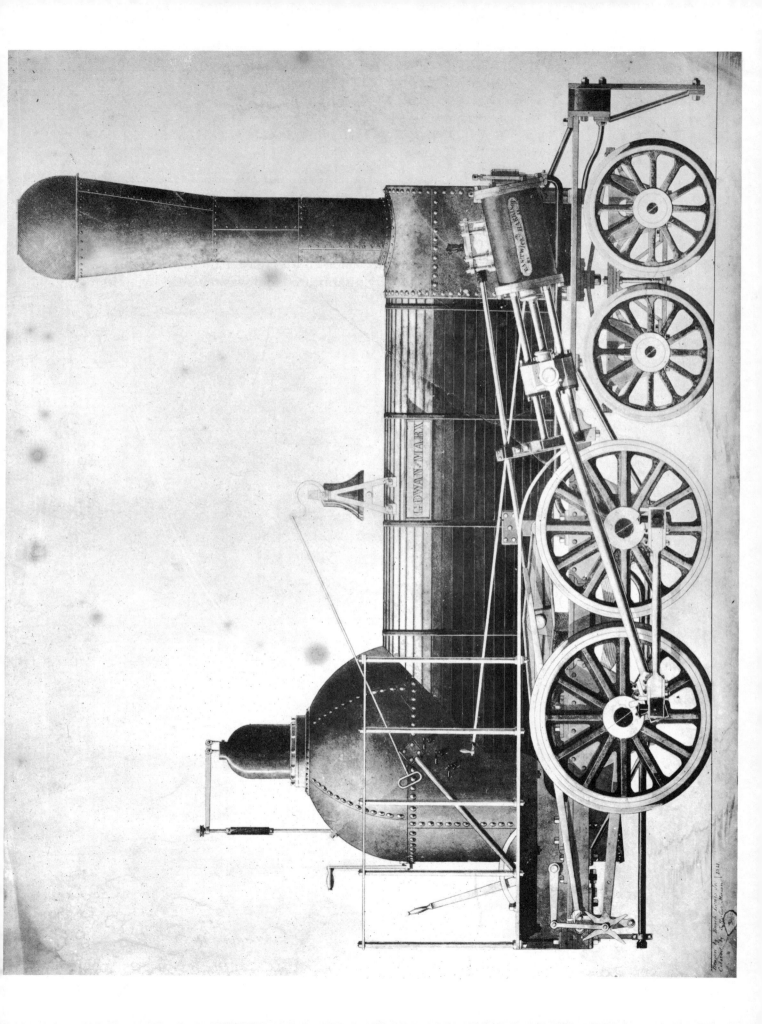

1840. BALDWIN'S 136th LOCOMOTIVE

BUILT for the Philadelphia, Germantown and Norristown Railroad, this was the first engine of Baldwin's which discarded the old wooden outside frame. The cylinders, truck, and pedestals for the driving wheels were attached directly to the boiler and thereafter the wood frame on subsequent engines gradually disappeared and was replaced by an iron one.

FOR a number of years after Campbell's and other eight-wheeled engines had proved satisfactory, especially in increased traction, Baldwin maintained that he did not believe there was any advantage in such a wheel arrangement. He did, however, give considerable thought to finding some means of increasing adhesion and the result was his patenting, in December, 1840, a geared engine. This was an adaptation of his standard 4–2–0 engine with coupling rods connected by cranks to a shaft on the leading truck. The shaft, in turn, was geared to the two axles, their cogwheels having wide teeth which remained meshed while still allowing the truck to pivot, the shaft remaining parallel with the driving axle. The gearing was, of course, proportionate with the driving wheel diameter so that the small wheels would revolve as much faster than the drivers as required.

This engine was finished in August, 1841, and later sold to the Sugar Loaf Coal Company. On a trial trip over the Philadelphia & Reading it hauled 590 tons from Reading to Philadelphia in 5 hours and 22 minutes. Very favorable comment resulted, both from railroad officials and the newspapers. The Committee on Science and Arts of the Franklin Institute made it the subject of a report which favored engines of this type for freight service. Strangely enough, despite all this publicity and its satisfactory service, no further call was made on Baldwin for such locomotives and it remained the only one of its kind he ever built.

Cylinders 13 by 16 inches   Weight 30,000 pounds   Drivers 44 inches in diameter Weight on drivers 11,775 pounds   Truck wheels 33 inches in diameter   Weight on truck 18,335 pounds

SIMILAR to the *Gowan & Marx*, but with an improved arrangement of mounting the leading truck, was this engine built by Eastwick & Harrison for the Baltimore & Ohio Railroad. The truck suspension consisted of a long spring on either side, to the ends of which were fastened the journals or axle boxes. The centers of the springs were held by a bolster upon which the forward part of the engine was supported. The driving wheels, too, were equalized.

In one year (1844) the *Mercury* traveled 37,000 miles, supposed to be the greatest mileage run by any engine up to that time. It was used in passenger service and was very fast, sometimes making a speed of 60 miles an hour.

The result of Eastwick & Harrison's remarkable success with the equalized driving wheel arrangement and consequent outstanding improvement in locomotive traction was a contract from the Russian Government to establish a locomotive works in that country. Soon after the *Mercury* and one other engine were completed, the Philadelphia Shops were closed and the equipment sent to Russia where the Alexandroffsky Head Mechanical Works were established.

Cylinders 14 by 20 inches   Driving wheels 60 inches in diameter

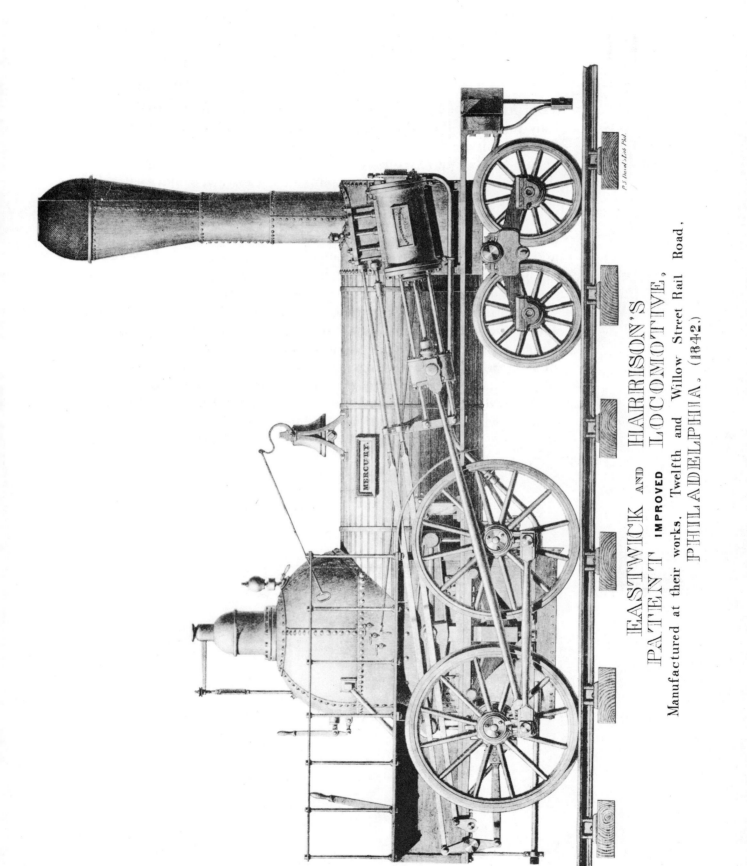

EASTWICK AND HARRISON'S
PATENT IMPROVED LOCOMOTIVE,

Manufactured at their works. Twelfth and Willow Street Rail Road,

PHILADELPHIA. (1842.)

P. S. Duval & Lith. Phil.

1842. BALDWIN'S SIX-WHEELS-CONNECTED ENGINE

THE problem of using all the weight of a locomotive for traction was not fully solved by the geared-truck machine and Baldwin determined to find the answer. The result was his flexible-beam truck engine, also known by the above name, which he patented in August, 1842. With this arrangement, the two front pairs of wheels could move laterally, their axles working in cylindrical, vertical pedestals. These were held by beams which could move independently of each other and of the engine's main frame. The rear pair of drivers was mounted as before and coupling rods connected all the wheels. The operation of the beams of the front truck was somewhat like that of a parallel ruler and permitted operation on curves without binding of any of the wheels.

The first engine thus built was completed in December, 1842, and sent to the Georgia Railroad. It was ordered by J. Edgar Thomson, then chief engineer and superintendent of the road, who later became president of the Pennsylvania Railroad. Its weight was 12 tons and in service it pulled a load of 250 tons up a grade of 36 feet to the mile.

So efficient was this locomotive and so well did it perform that many other orders soon followed from other roads, and for the next few years nearly every engine turned out of the Baldwin Works was of this type.

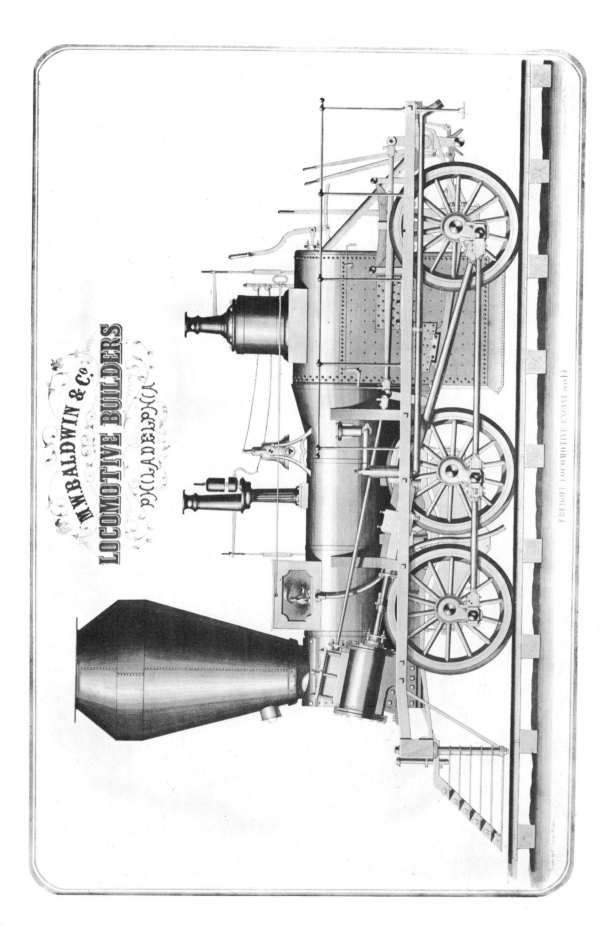

M.W.BALDWIN & Co.
LOCOMOTIVE BUILDERS
PHILADELPHIA

FREIGHT LOCOMOTIVE ENGINE No. D

THREE engines similar to that illustrated were built by William Norris for the Baltimore & Ohio Railroad. They were the *Pegasus*, Number 24, and the *Vesta*, Number 25, which were delivered in 1839, and the *Stag*, Number 31, which arrived in 1843. The design was much like that of Eastwick & Harrison's engines. The Norris advertising lithograph showing this type of engine says, "Wm. Norris & Co. Improved Eight Wheel Locomotive with Patent Flexible Truck. Manufactured at their works, Bush Hill, Philadelphia, 1843."

Cylinders 12 by 20 inches   Driving wheels 60 inches in diameter

WILLIAM NORRIS & CO IMPROVED EIGHT WHEEL LOCOMOTIVE.

THE first 0–8–0 engines, those having eight coupled wheels, on the Baltimore & Ohio Railroad were designed and built by Ross Winans. They were somewhat similar in cylinder and drive arrangement to the crabs, but were much larger and were the first Winans engines to have horizontal boilers. The appellation "mud digger" was derived from its pounding up the dirt from the light track then used, but each of the first twelve engines had its own name. That illustrated—the Number 37— is the *Cumberland* as it appeared in 1863.

These locomotives had main connecting rods coupled to cranks on a shaft extending across the frames behind the firebox, and this was geared to the rear axle. Their performance in service was exceptional and some were in use as late as 1865.

Cylinders 17 by 24 inches   Weight 47,000 pounds   Driving wheels 33 inches in diameter

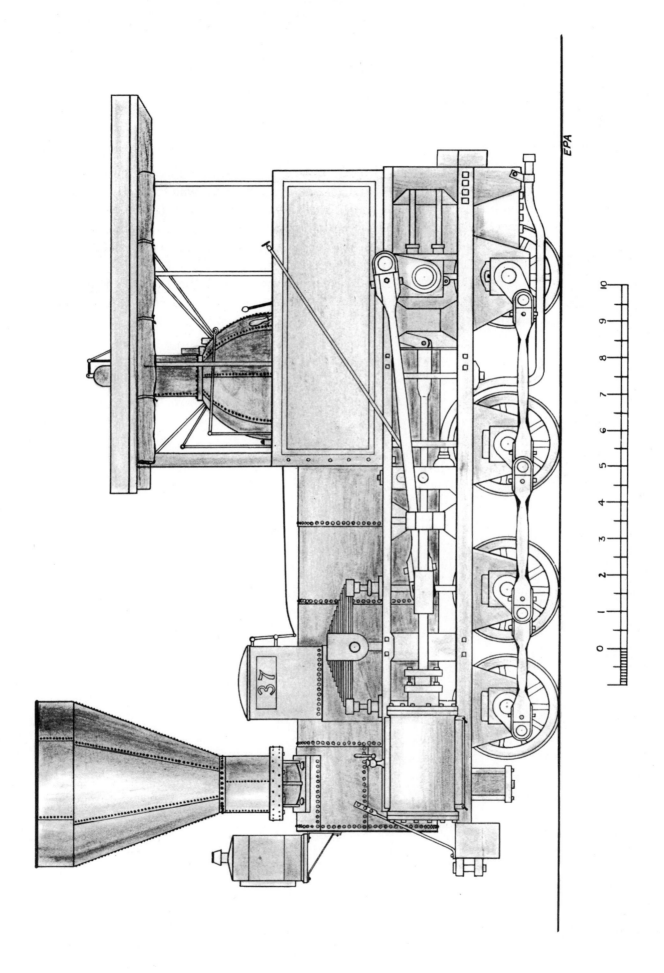

17 *1844. THE LION*

THE founder of the Hinkley & Drury firm was Holmes Hinkley who came from Maine. The first engine of their make was the *Cumberland*, which was finished in 1840. The *Lion* was delivered to the Nashua & Lowell Railroad in 1844. This was their twenty-second locomotive and, as the illustration shows, had some similarity to the *DeWitt Clinton*, although its boiler was somewhat larger.

The date usually given for the completion of the *Lion* is 1839, but since 1844 appears in Hinkley's own memoirs it is assumed to be the more correct of the two.

LION.

LOCOMOTIVE ENGINE, INTENDED FOR FREIGHT, HINKLEY & DRURY, BUILDERS, BOSTON, MASS.

A LATER type of Hinkley engine is this 4–4–0. Hinkley favored the inside cylinder arrangement and followed this practice for a number of years until the demand for outside connected engines caused the firm to do away with this type of construction. Though the print is dated 1846, it is possible that this engine may have been built later as the figures have been added subsequently.

No. 11.

LOCOMOTIVE ENGINE, HINKLEY & DRURY, BUILDERS, BOSTON, MASS.

THE first "ten wheeler" or 4–6–0 type was designed by Septimus Norris, a brother of William Norris. It was built by Richard Norris & Son in 1847 for the Philadelphia & Reading Railway and, when first delivered, caused some worry as to whether it would stay on the rails. The design was sound, however, and quite the reverse was true, the engine proving so satisfactory that the Pennsylvania Railroad ordered twenty of this type.

Cylinders 14½ by 22 inches   Weight 44,000 pounds   Driving wheels 46 inches in diameter

NORRIS BROTHERS 10 Wheel Freight Engine - Manufactured at their Works in PHILADELPHIA, PA.

P.S.Duval, Lith. Phila.

Drawn by Mr Uhlig Jr

A.Köllner, sculp.t

PATENT

ONE of the most distinctive classes of locomotives ever to be designed was the "camel" type of Ross Winans. Built in his shops for the Baltimore & Ohio Railroad, the first was placed in service in June, 1848, and marked a great advance in freight motive power. This, the Number 55, had a shorter and differently shaped firebox from that illustrated, which was built a few years later, but generally the characteristics were the same. The term "camel" is derived from the name of the first engine (others were *Iris,* Number 59; *Mars,* Number 61; *Phoenix,* Number 65; *Apollo,* Number 66; *Savage,* Number 68; *Pilot,* Number 69, etc.). Its appearance with the cab astride the boiler as well as its name originated the expression among B. & O. men of "riding on a camel's back."

The first engine of its type was followed by more than 200 turned out of the Winans shops during the next ten years, 119 of these being for the Baltimore & Ohio alone. They were also used on the Pennsylvania, Philadelphia & Reading, New York & Erie, and other roads. Shortly before the Civil War Winans closed his Baltimore Shops because no more orders were forthcoming from the Baltimore & Ohio and they were never permanently opened again. He sided (though passively) with the South and this may have influenced him. One of the most original and progressive of American locomotive builders, he was noted for his advocacy of heavier engines, building them and putting them to work on roads where light motive power had been the rule.

The first camel had 17 by 22-inch cylinders, weighed 45,000 pounds, and had 43-inch driving wheels. The later ones had cylinders generally 19 by 22 inches and weighed from 50,000 to 58,000 pounds, the wheel diameter being the same. Only the first and last pairs of wheels were flanged. The wheel base was 11 feet 3 inches.

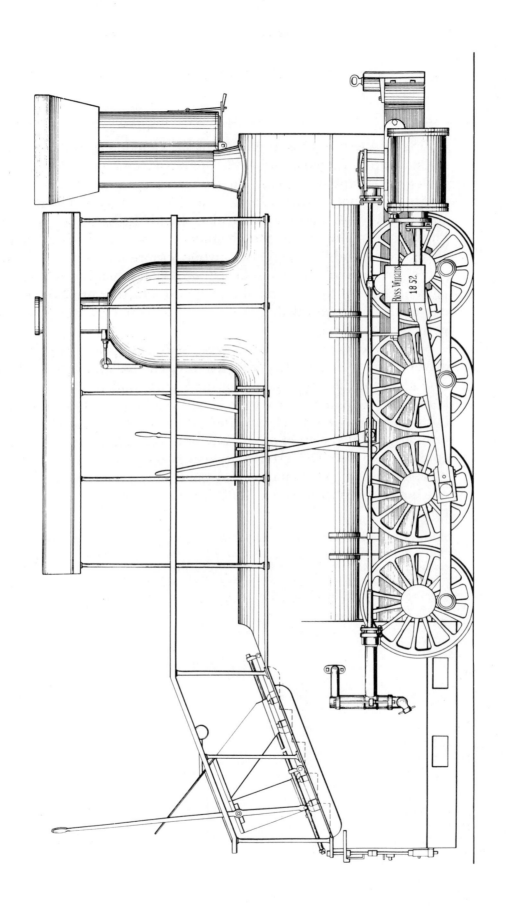

IN 1845 Robert Stevens, president of the Camden & Amboy Railroad, made a trip to England and while there was impressed with the large-drivered Crampton engines. On his return he asked Isaac Dripps to design a locomotive with a single pair of 8-foot drivers. The plans were approved in 1847 and the order placed with Richard Norris & Son of Philadelphia. The first engine, Number 28, was tried out on April 17, 1849. After it had been in service awhile, Dripps realized that the single pair of drivers did not have sufficient adhesion to haul satisfactorily the passenger trains then operated and opposed further use of this class of engine. He was overruled, however, and several more were built, some with smaller wheels

No sandboxes were provided and, with insufficient weight on the drivers, they were hard to get under way. The boiler, too, was not large enough to furnish ample steam for the large cylinders. The firedoor was below and behind the driving axle and the fireman stood in a pit, the bottom of which was level with the bottom of the ashpan. These engines ordinarily hauled a train of six cars, but even this was more than they could handle well. Once started, however, with a light train, they would go as fast as anyone would care to travel. They ran from 1849 to 1862, one being in service as late as 1865. Most had then been rebuilt as 4–4–0 types.

According to the order entered in the Norris books, the first engine had the following specifications: gauge, 4 feet 9⅞ inches; boiler, 38-inch diameter, made with spiral seams and to burn anthracite; cylinders, 13 by 54 inches; wheels, all of wrought iron, spaces between spokes filled with wood, drivers 96-inch diameter, leading wheels 36-inch diameter; weight not to exceed 50,000 pounds.

COAL BURNING PASSENGER LOCOMOTIVE ENGINE

"JOHN STEVENS"

BUILT BY MESSRS. NORRIS BROTHERS

PHILADELPHIA PA.

Side elevation.

Scale 3/4 of an inch to the foot.

Drawn by Wm. Cameron.

Engr by Ed. Herrlein.

T. Sinclair lith. 101 Chesnut st. Phila.

BALDWIN'S next improvement over his flexible-beam truck was to design an eight-wheeled engine, all of which would be drivers. To do this, the two rear pairs of wheels were mounted rigidly in the frame with the two front pairs made into a flexible-beam truck. The first engines of this type were built in 1846 when seventeen were made for the Philadelphia & Reading Railway. These, however, had the Bury style of boiler known as the "haystack," but in 1850 the wagon-top type replaced them. The engine illustrated is typical of the eight-drivered machines built about this year and for some years following and having the new type of boiler.

M.W.BALDWIN & Co.

LOCOMOTIVE BUILDERS

PHILADELPHIA

FREIGHT LOCOMOTIVE ENGINE

THIS is a representative engine of the Portland Company's Works built in 1851. It was furnished to the order of the Atlantic & St. Lawrence Railroad.

PORTLAND COS WORKS, PORTLAND, MAINE.

THE Boston Locomotive Works were the builders of this engine named the *Norwalk*. The Toledo, Norwalk and Cleveland Railroad acquired it in 1852.

JAMES F. HINKLEY DEL.

BOSTON LOCOMOTIVE WORKS,

HOLMES HINKLEY, Agent, N? 580 Harrison Avenue, BOSTON MASS.

J. H. Bufford's Lith. 762 Washington St. Boston

N? 5

BOSTON LOCOMOTIVE
WORKS 1852

THE *Irvington* was the first coal burner on the Hudson River Railroad. It was built by the Lawrence Machine Shop of Lawrence, Mass., to the specifications of A. F. Smith, superintendent of the railroad.

THE Lawrence Machine Shop for a few years in the fifties built a number of locomotives—as did other similar shops of that day. The New England states were then the center of manufacturing and naturally they expected their mechanics to secure a large part of the locomotive business. Most of the builders were content to follow current designs and gave little thought to improvements as long as they could furnish fairly good operating machines. They all entered the business for what money they could make, many as a side line to their regular shop or machinery business, and in consequence few contributions to the art resulted.

The engine illustrated is from a Lawrence advertising lithograph of 1853.

TWENTY-FIVE TON PASSENGER ENGINE.

LAWRENCE MACHINE SHOP
LAWRENCE MASS.

27 *1854. THE BELLE*

GENERALLY of this design were a number of eight-wheeled locomotives built by M. W. Baldwin & Co. in 1854. The *Belle* and *Flirt* were ordered by the Pennsylvania Railroad and were used in both freight and passenger service.

Driving wheels 72 inches in diameter

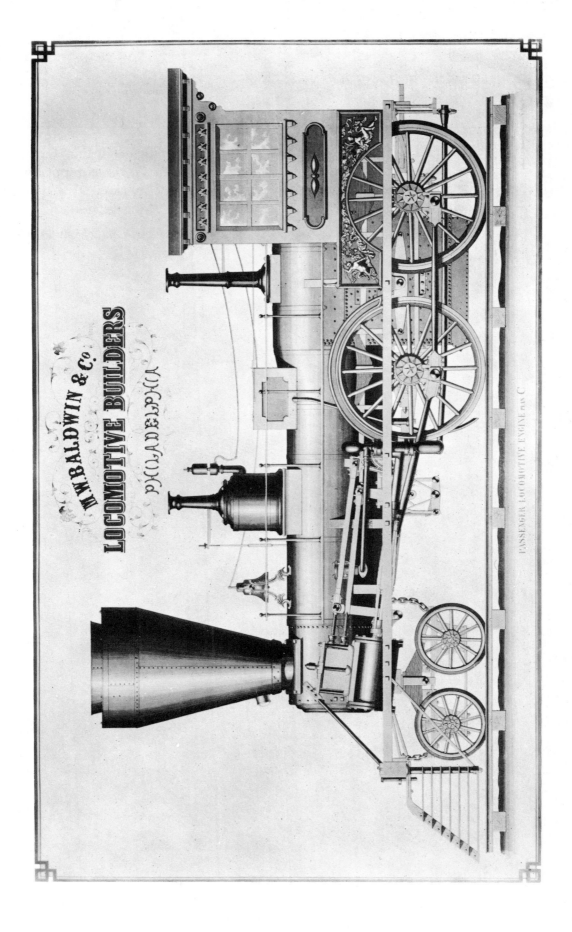

M.W.BALDWIN & Co.

LOCOMOTIVE BUILDERS

PHILADELPHIA

PASSENGER LOCOMOTIVE ENGINE no. C

ANOTHER Baldwin locomotive built for the Pennsylvania Railroad was this eight-coupled engine of 1854. The *Iron City* was equipped with the flexible-beam truck and was one of four of its class. This type of motive power was used for heavy freight and pushing service.

Cylinders 19 by 22 inches   Total weight 66,000 pounds   Driving wheels 43 inches in diameter

IRON CITY.

COAL BURNERS OF THIS PLAN WEIGHING FROM 50000 TO 64000 LBS.

M.W. BALDWIN & CO. LOCOMOTIVE BUILDERS,
PHILADELPHIA.

Lith. & Printed in Colors by L. N. Rosenthal Philadelphia.

Jonathan Ord Del.

A. LATHAM & Company was another New England firm of locomotive builders, their shop being located at White River Junction, Vermont. The *Competitor* was built for the Peoria & Oquawka Railroad in 1854.

LOCOMOTIVE & TENDER

BY JOHN P. LAIRD.

BUILT AT.

LATHAM & COs WORKS,

W. R. JUNCTION, VT.

COMPETITOR

SAMUEL HAYES, who was master of machinery for the Baltimore & Ohio Railroad from late in 1851 to the spring of 1856, was the designer of this class of engines. They followed generally the lines of Winans's camels but differed principally in having a four-wheeled leading truck, larger driving wheels, and several other improvements. They were known as the "Hayes's ten-wheelers" and were efficient and satisfactory both in passenger service, for which they were originally intended, and for moving freight. A number were built in the company's shops, seventeen being constructed up to 1860 alone. Though nine were built by various firms in 1853, the Number 198 was built in 1854 in the Mount Clare Shops.

In 1901 the last ten-wheel camel then in service, Number 173, traveled under its own power to Purdue University where it is now preserved with other old locomotives.

Cylinders 19 by 20 inches   Total weight 60,000 pounds   Driving wheels 50 inches in diameter   Rigid wheelbase 8 feet 8 inches   Weight on drivers 48,000 pounds Truck wheels 36 inches in diameter

Coal or Coke Burning Passenger Engine
by the
BALTIMORE & OHIO RAIL ROAD COMPANY
designed by
SAMUEL J. HAYES, MASTER-MACH'T

198

WEIGHT 60,000 LBS   SCALE 1 INCH 1 FOOT

Lith of A. Rosenthal, C'Phock S. 3d St Phila

1854. THE AUBURN

RICHARD NORRIS & Son built the *Auburn* for the Philadelphia & Reading Railway in 1854. It was used for passenger service and marks a considerable advance in design in the eight years since the *Chesapeake* was built for the same road.

RICHARD NORRIS & SON
BUILDERS
PHILADELPHIA.

EXPRESS ENGINE

LITH. IN COLORS, BY L. N. ROSENTHAL, PHIL.A

THE Trenton Locomotive Works were in existence only a few years, from 1853 to 1858. The company's partners were Van Cleve, McKean, and Dripps, the last being the same Isaac Dripps whose name we have already noted in connection with the Camden & Amboy and who later became superintendent of motive power for the Pennsylvania Railroad. The firm's first work was the construction of three Monsters for the Camden & Amboy.

The *Assanpink* was one of several engines built for the Belvidere Delaware Railroad. A novelty was the outside link motion which is evident in the illustration. This eliminated the cranked axle, which was otherwise necessary for operating the link motion.

TRENTON LOCOMOTIVE WORKS.

ASSANPINK

TO James Milholland must be attributed a large share of credit for his efforts in the locomotive's development. He had worked in Johnson's shop when Peter Cooper put his *Tom Thumb* together, and shortly after reaching the age of twenty-one he was appointed master mechanic of the Baltimore & Susquehanna Railroad (later the Northern Central). In 1848 he became master of machinery of the Philadelphia & Reading Railway. While there he experimented with various means of satisfactorily burning anthracite and in 1852 obtained a patent for a firebox to burn this fuel. During the same year his boiler, with some changes, was used in six locomotives built in the company's Reading Shops and known as the Pawnee class. The first of these was the *Wyomissing* and that illustrated, the *Juniatta,* was one of this type. The leading wheels, it may be noted, were not in a truck but were held rigidly in the frame.

These engines were used in freight service, particularly for what was known as the "coal trade."

Weight 26$\frac{9}{10}$ tons

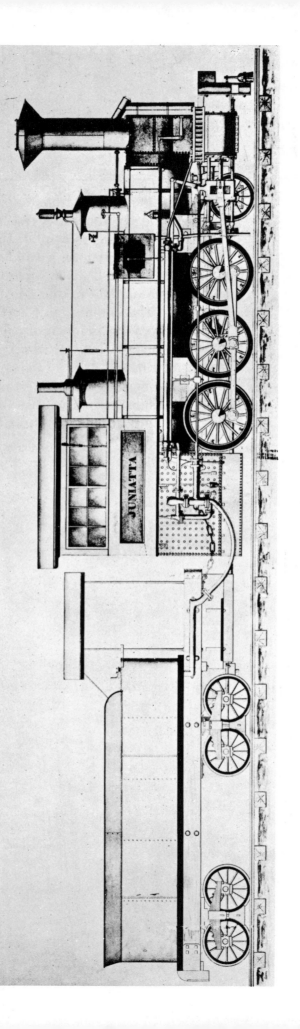

JAMES MILLHOLLAND'S ANTHRACITE COAL-BURNING LOCOMOTIVE

built at the

R. R. R. WORKS, READING, PA.

1855.

THE illustration taken from an original drawing is of the New York & Erie Railroad's Number 210. It was built by the New Jersey Locomotive & Machine Company in April, 1855.

These works were founded about 1845 as Swinburne, Smith & Co. and later John Brandt became superintendent of the firm. Zerah Colburn, another shining light in the industry, was mechanical engineer for several years. The engines built by the company were known as "Brandt engines" from the practice of calling locomotives after Baldwin, Wilmarth, Rogers, Hinkley, or whoever happened to be the particular firm's leading spirit.

The Number 210 is an interesting example of Erie motive power. Note such details as the unusual headlight bracket and pilot, as well as the extended runboard and handrail.

Cylinders 17 by 24 inches   Drivers 60 inches in diameter   Total weight 67,900 pounds (40,050 pounds on the drivers)

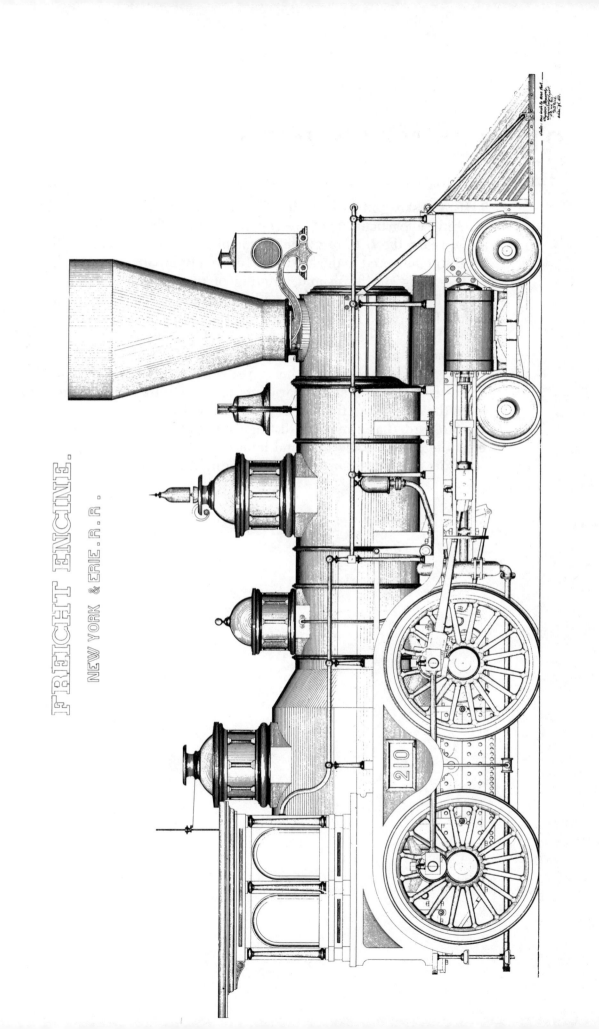

FREIGHT ENGINE.

NEW YORK & ERIE. R. R.

THE Amoskeag Manufacturing Company were well-known builders of machinery, particularly of fire engines. They built locomotives for only a few years, the *J. B. Jervis* being one of their last. It was completed in 1856 and delivered to the Northern Indiana Railroad.

Regarding the finish and painting of most engines of this period, Angus Sinclair said, "There was a great deal of ornamentation put upon some of the parts, but the effect on aesthetic taste was often grotesque where beauty was aimed at. Elaboration of brass in bands and coverings of domes, sand boxes, wheel covers, steam chests and cylinders with great vagaries of paint on other parts, conveyed the impression one receives from looking at the garments of an overdressed woman. Those were the days when the red smoke stack and vermilion painted wheels were regarded as a mark of distinguishing beauty. It was then considered the correct thing to spend hundreds of dollars on the painting of portraits or picturesque scenes on headlights, cab panels and tenders."

INSIDE CONNECTED PASSENGER ENGINE.

AMOSKEAG MANUFACTURING CO,

MANCHESTER N.H.

Wm. Amory Treasr.

C.W. Baldwin Agt.

THE *Nat Wright* is a representative locomotive turned out by the Cincinnati Locomotive Works in 1856. It was built for the Little Miami Railroad.

Unusual in the decorative treatment is the harp on the engine's headlight. The pilot, or "cowcatcher," too, is of a somewhat different design from most others of this period.

CINCINNATI LOCOMOTIVE WORKS.

MOORE & RICHARDSON, CINCINNATI.

A TYPICAL advertizing lithograph of the 1850's showing three classes of locomotives turned out by the Baldwin Shops of that period.

A Baldwin Advertizing Lithograph of the Fifties

THE Boston Locomotive Works, formerly Hinkley & Drury, built the *Rapid* for the Chicago, St. Paul & Fond du Lac Railroad in 1856. These works, known variously at later dates as Hinkley & Williams and the Hinkley Locomotive Works, continued in business until 1889.

HERE is another Amoskeag engine of 1858, the final year of their locomotive building. The lithograph is a typical one of its day and shows the company's buildings as well as a sample of their work.

OUTSIDE CONNECTED PASSENGER ENGINE.

AMOSKEAG MANUFACTURING CO.

MANCHESTER N. H.

Wm. Amory Treas.r
CITY EXCHANGE BOSTON MASS

C. W. Baldwin Agt.
MANCHESTER N. H.

JOHN BRANDT in the early days of the Philadelphia & Columbia Railroad was foreman of the road's shops (about 1834). He afterward was master machinist of the Georgia Railroad and later held the same position with the New York & Erie Railroad, which he left to become superintendent of the New Jersey Locomotive & Machine Works at Paterson. After some years there, he returned to his home town of Lancaster where he founded the Lancaster Locomotive Works about 1855.

The *John C. Breckenridge* is an excellent example of this company's work and was built for the Philadelphia & Columbia Railroad (though the name is reversed on some prints) the same year that the Pennsylvania Railroad purchased the state transportation system, including the Columbia Road.

PASSENGER LOCOMOTIVE

LANCASTER·PENN·LOCOMOTIVE WORKS, N.º ___ 1857.

JOHN BRANDT SEN.ʳ, GEN.ʳˡ SUPERINTENDENT.

JOHN BRANDT JUN.ʳ, ASS.ᵗ SUPERINTENDENT.

JAMES BLACK, PRESIDENT

M.G. KLINE, TREASURER.

JOHN C. BRECKENRIDGE

WILLIAM MASON started in the business of locomotive building in 1852 at Taunton, Mass. His engines were handsome without overdoing the ornamentation practiced by other builders and he liked and took an interest in his work. This is evidenced by his statement:

My principal business has been making cotton machinery. At the time I commenced locomotive building, there was a little slackness in cotton machinery, and for that reason I took hold of locomotives. My locomotive business is now the meanest part of it and always was. I took an interest in it and tell my friends that I got up locomotives for fun, but that it was the most expensive fun I ever had. I make just enough money from my cotton machinery to make up the losses on locomotives.

The *Phantom* is an excellent example of the kind of work Mason produced in 1857. The original lithograph's colors are unusual in that they are predominantly blue, rather than the greens and reds common in contemporary prints.

120

W. MASON & Cᵒ BUILDERS, TAUNTON, MASS.

THE Niles Locomotive Works were founded in 1852 by two brothers—Jonathan and James Niles—and Coleman Sellers, another well-known pioneer railroad mechanical engineer, shortly afterward became their shop foreman. Niles engines were used on a number of roads and performed well. Less than ten years after the firm's founding, however, the brothers retired and moved to Hartford.

The *Queen City* was a typical engine of their construction but it is not known to what railroad it was delivered.

EXPRESS ENGINE

Drawn and Designed for

NILES & CO.

CINCINNATI.

BY JOHN L. WHETSTONE.

QUEEN CITY.

1858. THE FASHION

THE *Fashion* is a representative engine constructed by the Boston Loco-motive Works in 1858. Note that while Plate 38 indicates Holmes Hinkley as "agent," according to this he is "president" of the firm.

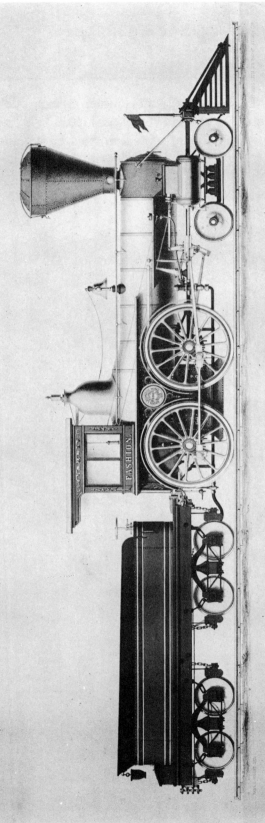

BOSTON LOCOMOTIVE WORKS,

(FORMERLY HINKLEY & DRURY,) Nº 380 HARRISON AVENUE, BOSTON, MASS.

Holmes Hinkley
PRESIDENT.

O.W.Bayley
PRINCIPAL OF MECHANICAL DEPARTMENT.

M. W. BALDWIN & Co. were the builders of the *President*. It was delivered to the Cleveland & Pittsburgh Railroad in 1859. In general arrangement, despite its being a "ten wheeler," there is much reminiscent of the *Tiger* in this Baldwin design. The raised, square sandbox with the bell above is a peculiarity of many of these early Pennsylvania Railroad locomotives.

M. W. BALDWIN & C°.,

LOCOMOTIVE BUILDERS

PHILADELPHIA.

Jonathan Ord, Del.

On Stone by Max Rosenthal

Lith. & Printed in Colors by L. N. Rosenthal, Cor 4th & Chestnut Sts. Phila.

THE *Hiawatha* and her sister engine, the *Minnehaha*, of the Philadelphia & Reading were designed by James Milholland. They were built in the company's Reading Shops in 1859 and intended for passenger service, in which they were used until 1867. The *Hiawatha* was later used on the Lebanon Valley and East Pennsylvania Railroads. By having traveled 720,727 miles, 51,000 of these in 1880, toward the end of that year it set up a new mileage record for motive power on the Reading. The *Hiawatha* was taken out of service in 1883.

Weight 25²⁄₁₀ tons

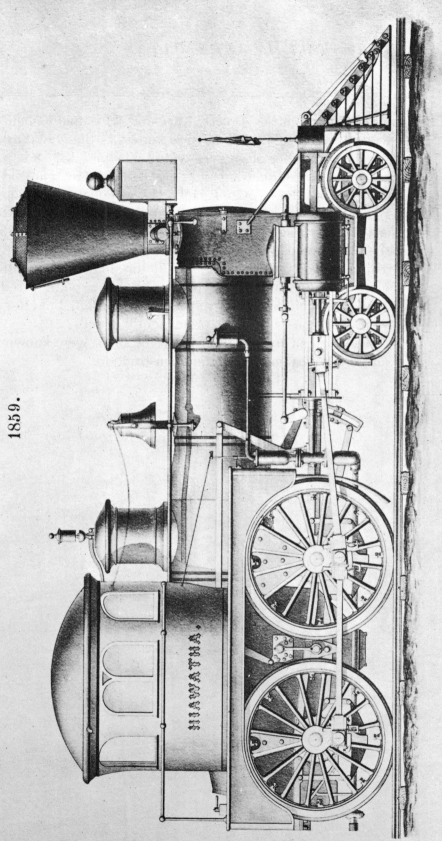

JAMES MILLHOLLAND'S

Anthracite Coal Burning Passenger Locomotive

1859.

HIAWATHA.

W. Tamerer del.

EARLY in the fifties, Breese, Kneeland & Company opened locomotive works in Jersey City which were known as the New York Locomotive Works. A number of engines were built until 1857 when the financial panic forced their closing and they then were reorganized as the Jersey City Locomotive Works. In 1865 the works were rented to James Mc-Henry. His intention was to build engines for the Atlantic & Great Western Railway, rather than purchase them from other builders who were then busy with government orders on account of the Civil War. Over a hundred locomotives were built for this road and then the works closed in 1867. In 1869 the Jersey City Shops were leased to Nathaniel McKay, son of the famous shipbuilder of Boston, but after a few engines were built the works were permanently closed.

The *Jersey City* was built when the shops were known by that name and is a typical engine of their construction.

JERSEY CITY

FOR THE AMERICAN RAILWAY REVIEW.

ENDICOTT & CO. LITH. N.Y.

THIS engine is especially notable in that it was the first in America to have its boiler made entirely of steel, or as it was called in contemporary accounts, "homogenous metal." It was built at the Hamilton Works of the Great Western Railway of Canada. An extract from the Annual Reports of the company says:

13th February 1861   Richard Eaton, Locomotive
                                                                    Superintendent

During the half year, we have completed two more new and powerful freight engines & tenders, the "Scotia" and "Erin," and they have commenced work most satisfactorily, their boilers are made of the best semi-steel or homogenous metal and are double riveted. The driving and tender wheels are wrought iron forged at the Company's Works in Hamilton and are the first wheels of the kind ever made in Canada. The two new freight engines abovementioned with their tenders cost $22,009.

The steel used in the boiler was imported from England and cost 16 cents a pound. The weight of the boiler without tubes was 10,356 pounds and with tubes the weight was 14,999 pounds. The working pressure was 130 pounds. The engines burned coal originally but, due to its scarcity on account of the Civil War, they were changed to wood burners and balloon stacks replaced the straight type.

Cylinders 16 by 24 inches   Total weight 69,440 pounds   Driving wheels 60 inches in diameter   Gauge 5 feet 6 inches

PROBABLY the most famous name in connection with locomotive building in New Jersey is that of Thomas Rogers. In 1832, after a few years
of making looms in Paterson, he became head of the new firm of Rogers,
Ketchum & Grosvenor. In 1835 the company announced it would undertake the construction of locomotives and other railroad equipment. The
Sandusky was its first engine, completed in 1837 (see page 33) and
its first American type was built in 1844. Thomas Rogers died in 1856
but the firm continued as the Rogers Locomotive Works.

Typical of the work turned out in the early sixties is the engine illustrated. It is very similar to the famous *General* of Civil War fame.

COAL BURNING FREIGHT ENGINE

Rogers L. & M. Works.

THOMAS ROGERS

R.L. & M.W.

THE Atlantic & Great Western Railway's main line was from Salamanca, N. Y., to Dayton, with a branch line to Cleveland. It formed a through broad gauge (6 feet) route from New York to St. Louis via the Erie Railway to Salamanca, the Atlantic & Great Western to Dayton, the Cincinnati, Hamilton & Dayton to Cincinnati and thence over the Ohio and Mississippi from Cincinnati to St. Louis.

Number 16 was built by Danforth, Cooke & Company and is typical both of the motive power of the Civil War period and of this road's locomotives about the time of its completion.

Note that the letter "W" was omitted by the artist from the tender lettering.

The Number 16 had 54-inch driving wheels and cylinders 16 by 22 inches. It weighed 62,000 pounds and was intended for freight service

THE first engine to be built with six pairs of driving wheels was the *Pennsylvania,* designed by James Milholland and completed at the Philadelphia & Reading Shops in 1863. It was intended and used for pusher service, particularly in handling coal trains over the summit of the hills between the Schuylkill and Delaware Rivers.

Though originally both fuel and water were carried on the engine, when it was rebuilt in 1870, with the rear pair of drivers omitted, a separate tender was attached. The principal reason for its being modified was because it had difficulty in negotiating curves, some of which were as short as 320-foot radius. It was so powerful that it was destructive to the light cars then used for handling coal.

Cylinders 20 by 26 inches   Weight 100,300 pounds   Driving wheels 43 inches in diameter   Wheelbase 19 feet 7 inches

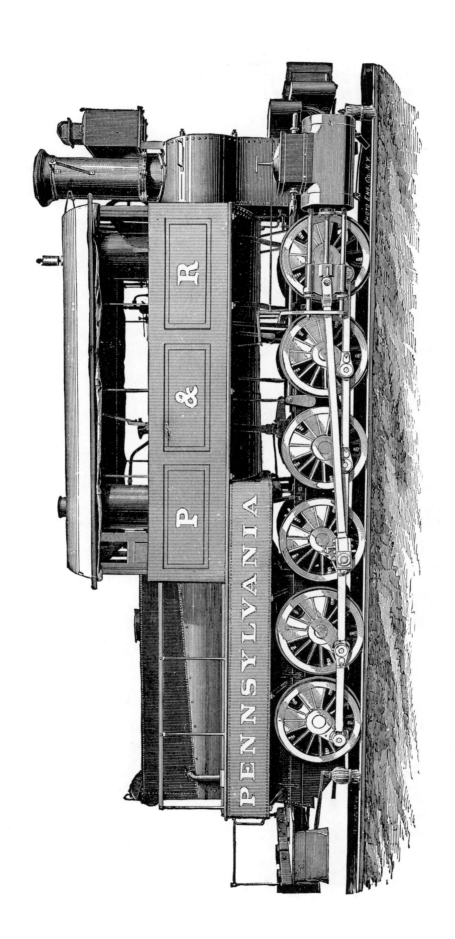

51 *1864. 4-4-0 TYPE*

THE Hinkley & Williams Works of Boston built this engine in 1864. It was made for the Peninsular Railroad of Wisconsin.

HINKLEY AND WILLIAMS WORKS, BOSTON, MASS.

416 HARRISON AVENUE.

THE New York & Harlem Railroad obtained this locomotive from the Taunton Locomotive Works in 1865. It will be noted that the headlight was not on its bracket when the drawing was made. Often such accessories were supplied by the railroad and not by the builders.

THIS Mason engine built for the Cape Cod Central Railroad in 1867 typifies perhaps the acme of locomotive design as practiced in the sixties. As M. N. Forney, one of the outstanding authorities on motive power, once said of William Mason, "He was a wonderfully ingenious man and combined with his ingenuity a high order of the artistic sense, so that his work was always most exquisitely designed. It might be said of his locomotives that they are 'melodies cast and wrought in metal.'" Attention may be called to the very unusual tender trucks on this engine.

The Cape Cod Central later became part of the Old Colony Railroad, which in turn the New Haven leased for a long term.

THE name McKay was a famous one in New England and, for that matter, everywhere in shipping circles. Few people have not heard of Donald McKay of clipper-ship fame. But hardly any of these same persons know that his son Nathaniel contributed to land transportation in that his firm built locomotives as well as ships and machinery. The McKay & Aldus Iron Works of East Boston built this engine in 1868. In 1869 McKay tried reopening the old Jersey City Locomotive Works, but very little business was obtained and they soon closed.

McKAY & ALDUS IRON WORKS, EAST BOSTON, MASS.

MANUFACTURE LOCOMOTIVE ENGINES & TENDERS, MARINE ENGINES,
IRON & WOODEN STEAM SHIPS, SUGAR MILLS, MACHINERY, &c &c

THE first of the Pennsylvania Railroad's Class C locomotives was built in 1869 at the Altoona Shops. Others of this type were added to the road's motive power for several years and they were the standard passenger locomotives until the eighties. According to the new classification of motive power on the Pennsylvania, this particular type was known as the D3. Most engines of this class had wagon-top boilers.

In connection with this class of locomotive, it is interesting to note that experiments were made in 1870 with track tanks for taking water by means of scoops on engine tenders. Three years later they were put into regular service and Class C engines used this system for taking water.

Cylinders 17 by 24 inches   Total weight 79,100 pounds   Driving wheels 62 inches in diameter   Weight on drivers 50,950 pounds   Total wheelbase 22 feet 5⅝ inches   Rigid wheelbase 8 feet 6 inches   Tractive force 11,890 pounds

J.H. GEISSEL. DEL.

THE six-wheel engine illustrated was built by the Baldwin Locomotive Works for switching service on the Baltimore & Potomac Railroad. This illustration and the others of 1870 that follow are reproduced from Weissenborn's book of locomotive drawings of that date.

Wheelbase 10 feet   Driving wheels 43 inches in diameter

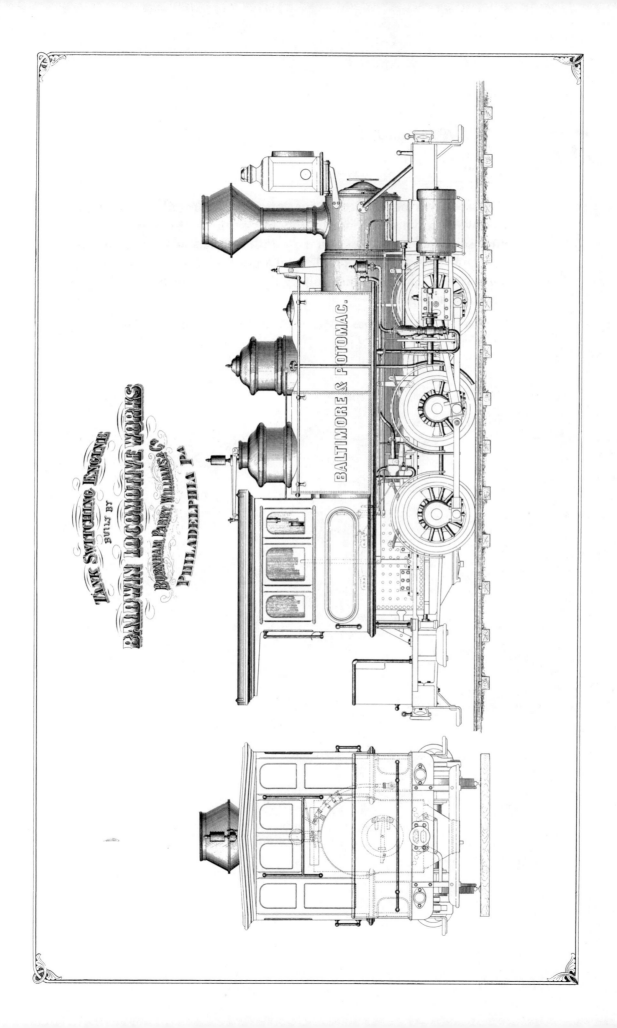

TANK SWITCHING ENGINE
BUILT BY
BALDWIN LOCOMOTIVE WORKS
BURNHAM, PARRY, WILLIAMS & C.º
PHILADELPHIA Pª

BALTIMORE & POTOMAC.

THE *Star* was not a locomotive intended for regular service but was what was known as a "superintendent's engine." It was designed for the purpose of making inspection trips with railroad officials. The cab had a seating arrangement which allowed a good view of the track for a number of riders. The *Star* was built by the Central Railroad of New Jersey's Elizabethport Shops.

Cylinders 11 by 15 inches   Wheelbase 22 feet 2¼ inches   Drivers 54 inches in diameter

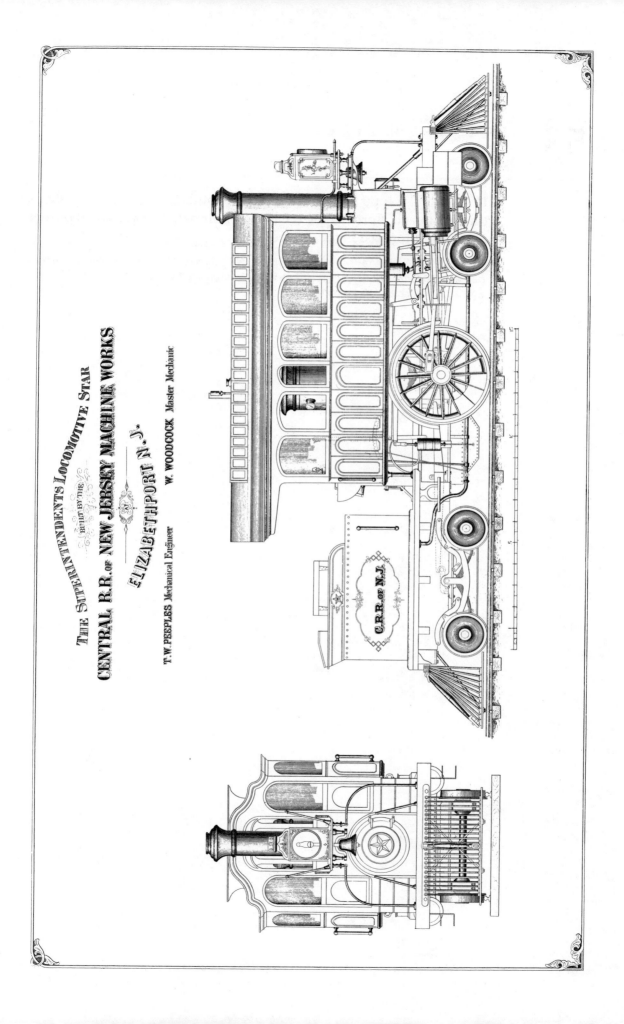

The Superintendents Locomotive Star

BUILT BY THE

CENTRAL R.R. of NEW JERSEY MACHINE WORKS

ELIZABETHPORT N.J.

T. W. PEEPLES Mechanical Engineer   W. WOODCOCK Master Mechanic

C.R.R. of N.J.

THIS American type of 4–4–0 engine was built by the company shops of the Pittsburgh, Fort Wayne & Chicago Railroad. It was a wood burner and was used for passenger service.

Cylinders 16 by 24 inches   Total weight 65,295 pounds   Driving wheels 66 inches in diameter for passenger engine, 60 inches in diameter for freight engine   Weight on driving wheels 41,440 pounds

PITTSBURG, FORT WAYNE & CHICAGO RAILWAY CO.

WESTERN DIVISION.

STANDARD PASSENGER and FREIGHT LOCOMOTIVE

BUILT AT THE COMPANY'S WORKS.

JAMES M. BOON   MASTER MECHANIC

FORT WAYNE, INDIANA.

A F Schoenhein del.

59 *1870. 2-4-2 TYPE*

THE Grant Locomotive Works were the builders of this engine intended for suburban or light passenger service. It burned anthracite and was built for the Central Railroad of New Jersey.

Cylinders 14 by 22 inches   Wheelbase 22 feet 8½ inches (7 feet, rigid)   Driving wheels 56 inches in diameter

ANTHRACITE COAL BURNING LOCOMOTIVE

BUILT BY THE

GRANT LOCOMOTIVE WORKS

PATERSON N.J.

AN example of a Baldwin-built Mogul, this engine is typical of freight motive power in the early seventies.

Total wheelbase 21 feet 9¾ inches   Driving wheels 54 inches in diameter   Rigid wheelbase 14 feet 6 inches   Leading wheels 30 inches in diameter

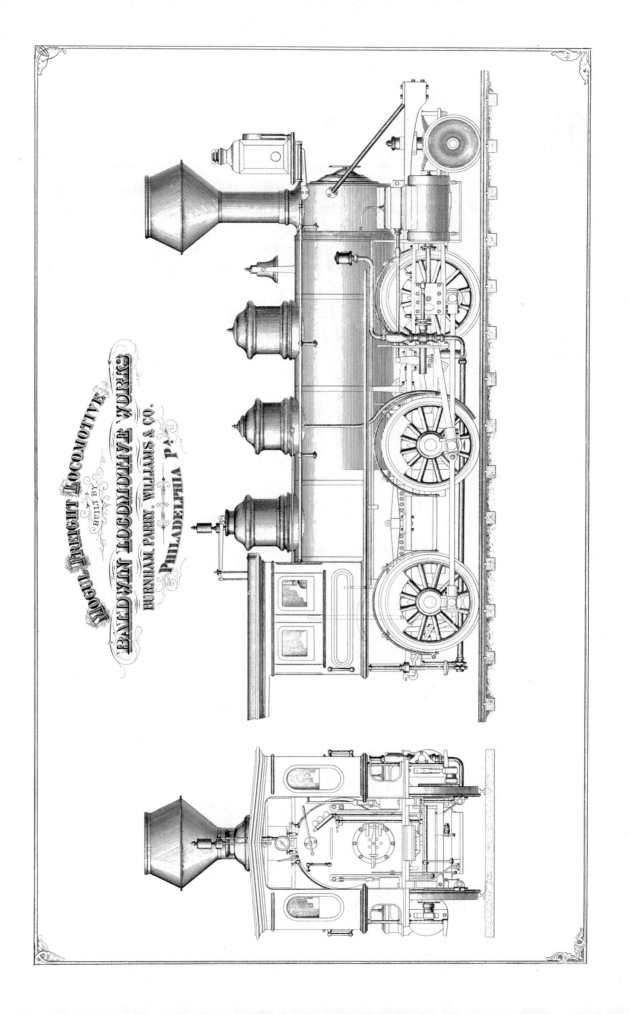

MOGUL FREIGHT LOCOMOTIVE

BUILT BY

BALDWIN LOCOMOTIVE WORKS

BURNHAM PARRY, WILLIAMS & CO.

PHILADELPHIA PA.

ANOTHER Mogul type or 2–6–0 was this coal-burning engine built by the Danforth Locomotive & Machine Works and intended for moving freight.

Cylinders 18 by 20 inches   Weight 59,720 pounds   Driving wheels 42 inches in diameter   Total wheelbase 19 feet 9 inches   Rigid wheelbase 6 feet 9 inches

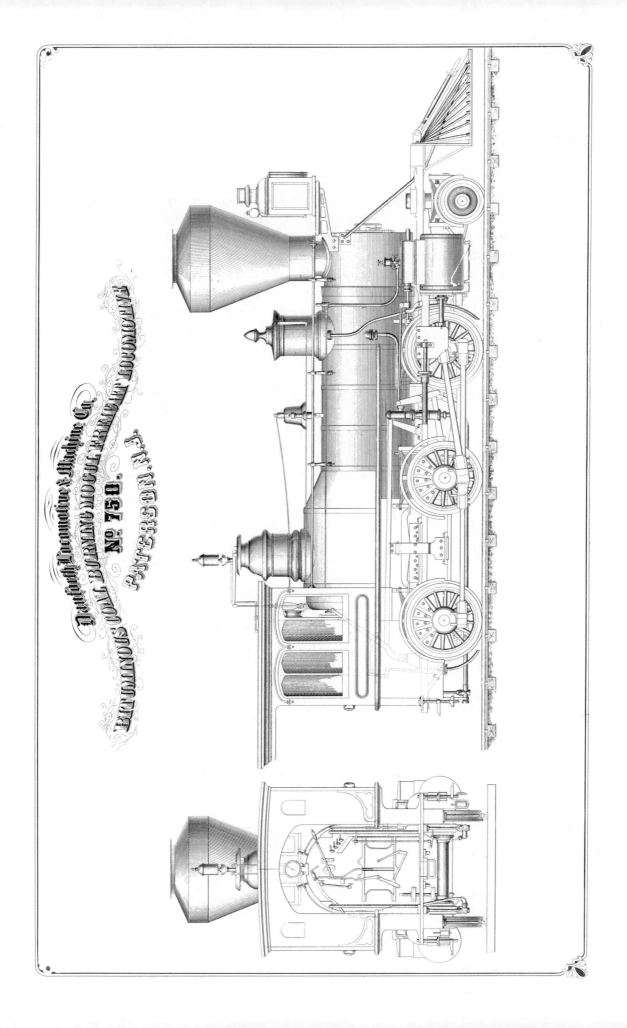

Danforth Locomotive & Machine Co.

BITUMINOUS COAL BURNING MOGUL FREIGHT LOCOMOTIVE

No 750.

PATTERSON, N.J.

NOT much seems to be known about this Rogers design for a 2–8–4 tank locomotive. It was probably intended for heavy traffic on short runs. The design, being well proportioned, is typical of Rogers. It should be noted that this may have been the first Berkshire type, an engine of a 2–8–4 wheel arrangement, though this term is more correctly applied to locomotives of this plan with tenders. Most of this class of "double-enders" were built for narrow-gauge freight roads.

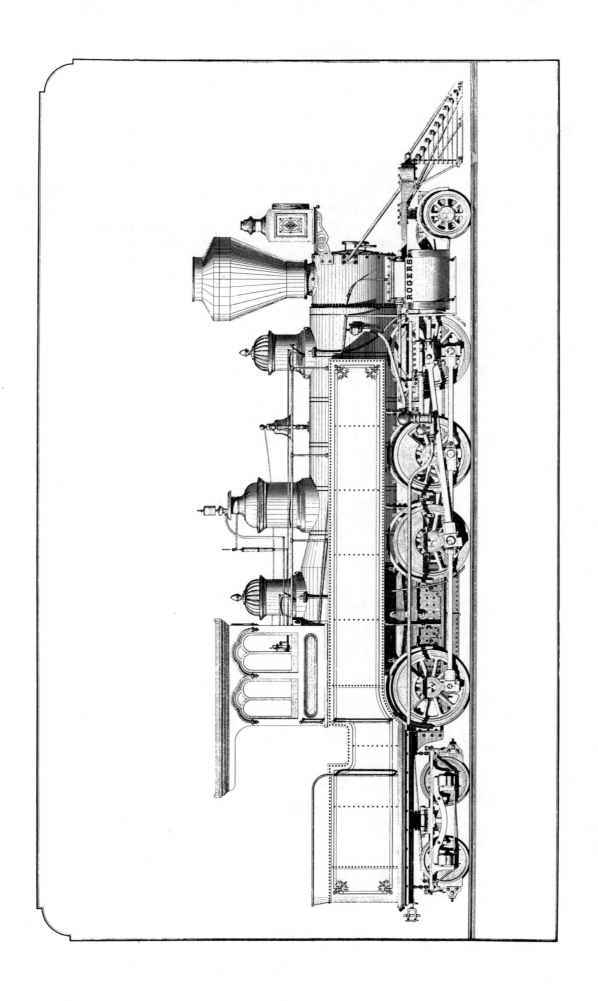

63 *1872. 4-4-0 NUMBER 179*

THE New York Central Railroad used engines of this general type in passenger service in the seventies. The Number 179 was built at the company's Rochester Shops and is not very much different from the Number 110 (Plate 65).

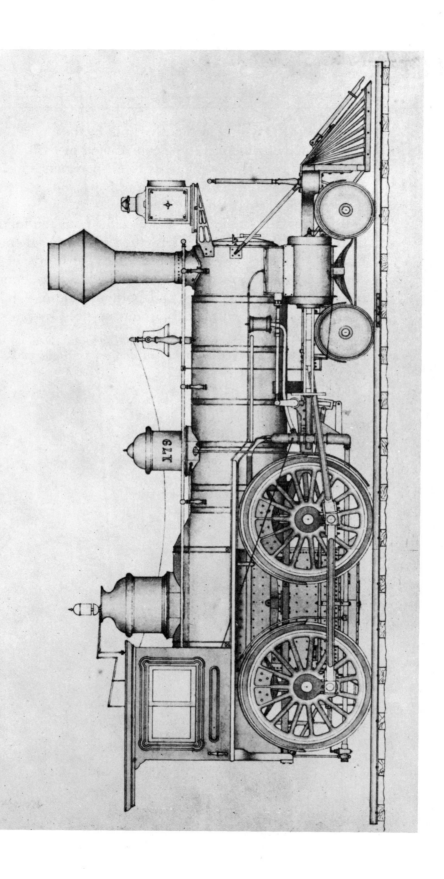

A STANDARD type of locomotive built by the Grant Locomotive Works is this 4–4–0 or American type constructed in 1873. While the builders' description is fairly complete as to all pertinent mechanical data, the road which obtained it is not given. Nevertheless it is typical both of the year and of this company's work.

It is interesting to note in the specifications the following, as it gives us an idea of the pains taken with the appearance of engines of that day: Finish—cylinders neatly cased with brass; heads of cast iron; steam chests with cast iron tops, bodies cased with brass; dome with brass casing on body and brass top and bottom moldings; boiler lagged with wood and covered with Russian iron, secured by brass bands polished.

Cylinders 16 by 24 inches   Weight 62,000 pounds   Driving wheels 61 inches in diameter   Truck wheels 28 inches in diameter   Rigid wheelbase 8 feet   Total wheelbase 21 feet 9 inches

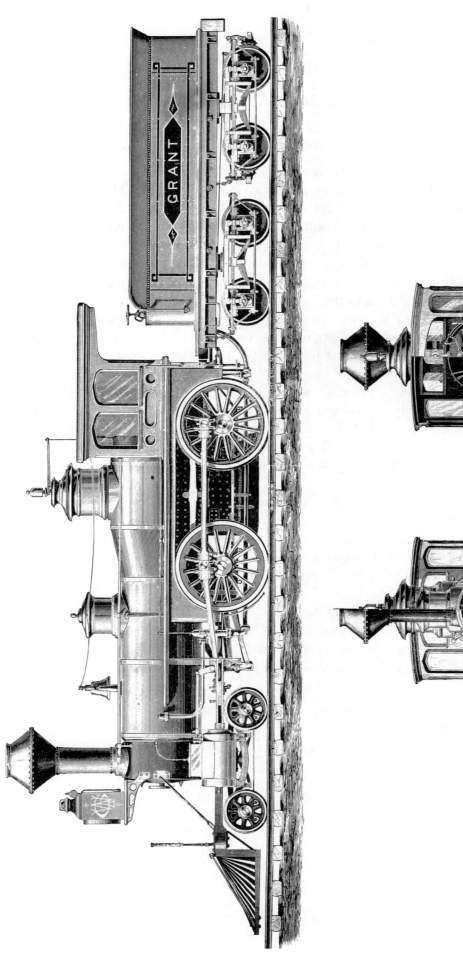
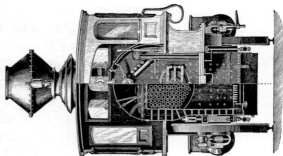
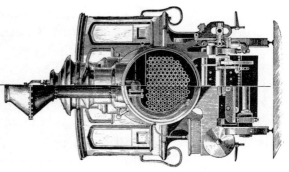

AN example of New York Central power in the seventies is this 4–4–0 of 1874, which was built by Mr. Watkeys at Syracuse. This is the engine which was used a year later to haul the fast mail train between Syracuse and Buffalo and which attained the then astonishing speed of 65 to 75 miles an hour. This high-speed running was the subject of an article in *Harper's Weekly* (November 27, 1875), which claimed that "the performances of this engine are so remarkable that she—engines, like ships, are always of the feminine gender—deserves to have her portrait in *Harper's Weekly*, and to have the story of her exploits told."

For nine consecutive Sundays in this year the experiment of running a Sunday newspaper train between New York and Buffalo, over 470 miles, was successfully carried out. The average speed was 50 miles an hour and even railroad officials were at first skeptical and uneasy about the safety of the scheduled operation. The first trip, therefore, upon which depended the success and continuation of the experiment, was the most interesting. This occurred on the morning of July 4 and was made in collaboration with the New York *Herald,* which newspaper the train carried.

Engine Number 110 was coupled on at Syracuse and brought the train into Buffalo five minutes ahead of time.

As a result of the example set by the *Herald* train, the first "fast mail" on the New York Central and Lake Shore railroads was run on September 16 of that year. There were four mail cars, each named after the governors of states and a "palace" car. It was drawn by engine Number 57 and averaged 50 miles an hour, reaching Buffalo in 11 hours and 15 minutes. "The process of catching the mail-bags from the cranes set up on the side of the track was watched with much interest. When the mail-sack was unusually heavy, a perceptible shock was felt throughout the car as it was hooked on the arm of the iron catcher."

The 110 had 17-inch diameter cylinders with a 24-inch stroke. Her driving wheels were 73 inches in diameter.

ENGINE Number 600, the *J. C. Davis*, was the first passenger service engine of the Mogul or 2–6–0 type to be used on the Baltimore & Ohio Railroad. It was designed and built in 1875 by John C. Davis, then master of machinery at the company's Mount Clare Shops, and exhibited at the Centennial Exposition the following year, where it was known as the largest engine yet made. The service for which it was intended was hauling mail and express trains over what was then the Third Division from Keyser to Grafton, 78¾ miles. With a five-car train of about 114-ton total weight, the scheduled time made over the Division was 3 hours notwithstanding heavy grades of 116 to 125 feet per mile between Piedmont and Altamount.

Cylinders 19 by 26 inches   Total weight 90,400 pounds   Driving wheels 60 inches in diameter   Weight on drivers 76,550 pounds   Truck wheels 31 inches in diameter   Rigid wheelbase 15 feet 1 inch   Total wheelbase 22 feet 11 inches

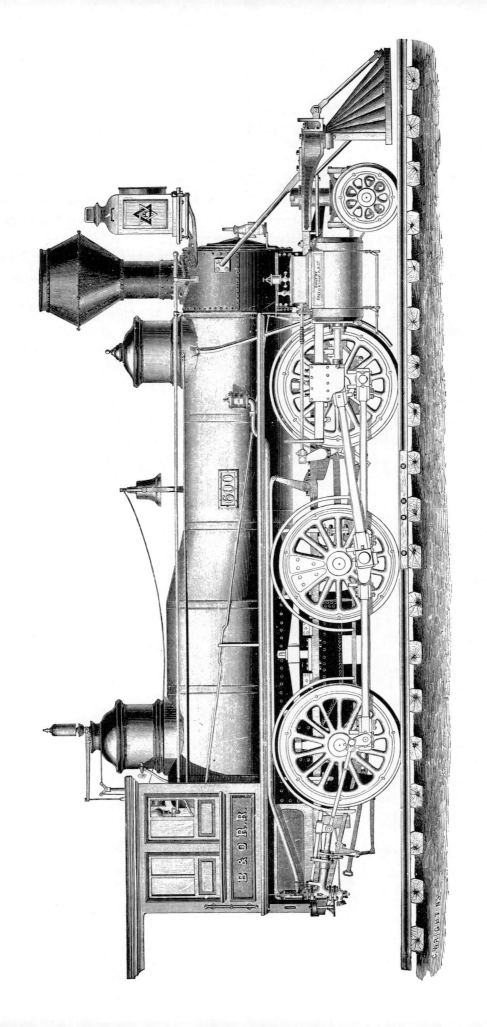

NUMBER 26 of the New York & Harlem Railroad was built by the Schenectady Locomotive Works. It was delivered in 1876 and put into suburban passenger service.

Matthias N. Forney, from whom this type of engine takes its name, patented the design in 1866. The wheel arrangement was intended to combine the advantage of the maximum weight of the engine on the driving wheels (for traction) with the easy riding obtained with the engine truck but eliminating the tender. Thus, as built, such engines had the principal weight on the drivers, and the weight of what would otherwise be carried by the tender was on the truck. A number of other points were claimed by the designer, such as better visibility, less cinders and smoke carried into the cab, and shorter over-all length.

Though the illustration seems to indicate a separate tender, it can be attributed to the angle at which the drawing was made, as actually the engine frame was carried through to the rear of the coal bunker.

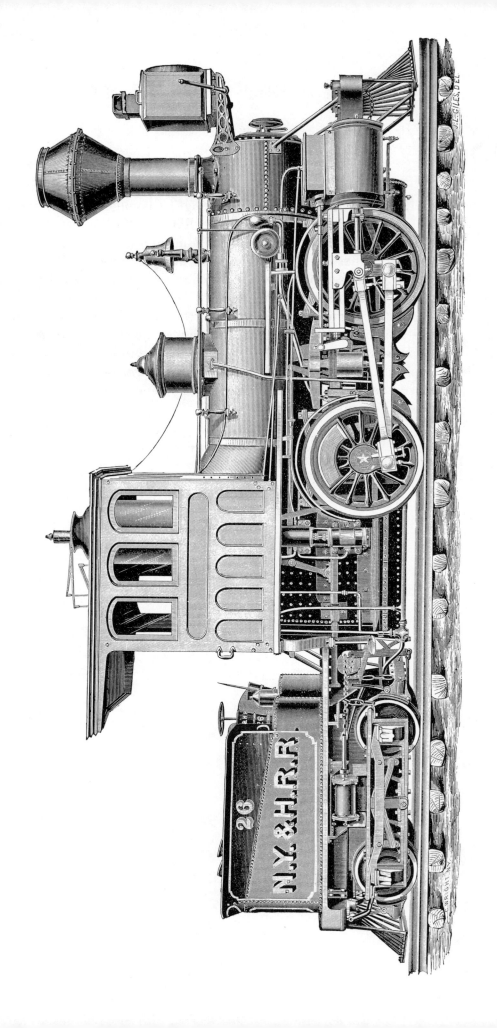

THIS type of small locomotive for light passenger service was built in 1877 for the Metropolitan Elevated Railroad by the Grant Locomotive Works. The entire engine was enclosed in a cab similar to a small car body and these engines were known as "dummies." They were the first engines used on the road and were superseded by the Forney type shortly after the line was opened.

When the wheel arrangement of the locomotives to be used on this line was first being considered, there was considerable discussion as to the merits of having small leading wheels to guide the engine going into small radius curves. These were decided upon but most were later removed as they were found unnecessary. The illustration shows the engines as originally built.

Cylinders 10 by 16 inches   Total weight 32,500 pounds   Driving wheels 30 inches in diameter   Weight on drivers 27,500 pounds   Truck wheels 28 inches in diameter   Total wheelbase 15 feet 6 inches

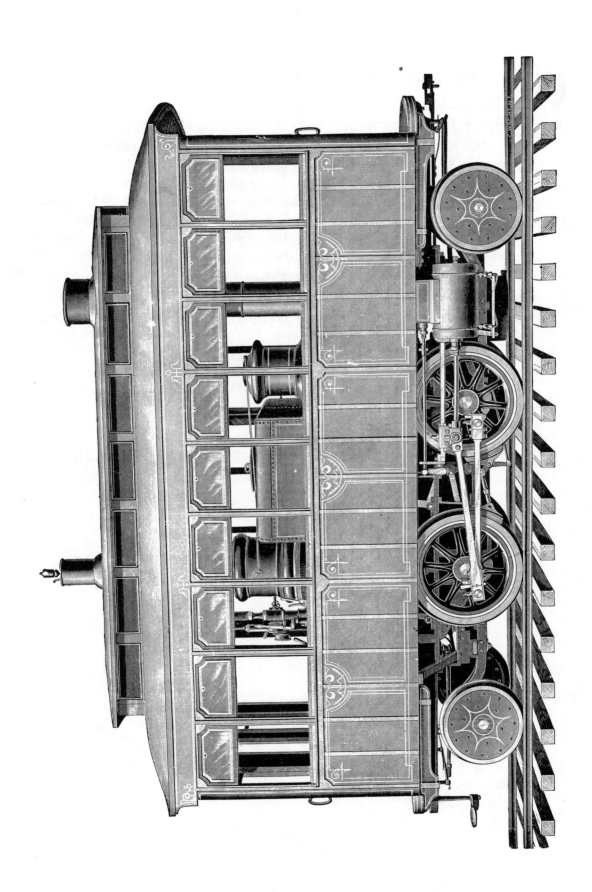

SEVERAL locomotive builders contributed motive power to the New York Elevated Railroad. The Forney type, more than any other, is typical of the kind of engines used. All the elevated lines also employed these engines and they could operate over reverse curves of 119-foot radius. Over one hundred were in use by the early eighties and this number had increased to more than three times as many by the late nineties, when the elevated lines handled more trains than any other railroad in the world. Similar locomotives, but of larger dimensions, were built subsequent to 1878, when that illustrated was put in service.

Cylinders 10 by 14 inches to 10 by 16 inches   Total weight 29,890 to 35,140 pounds
On drivers 19,170 to 23,790 pounds   Driving wheel diameter 38 and 42 inches
Fuel anthracite   Driving wheelbase 5 feet   Tank capacity 450 gallons

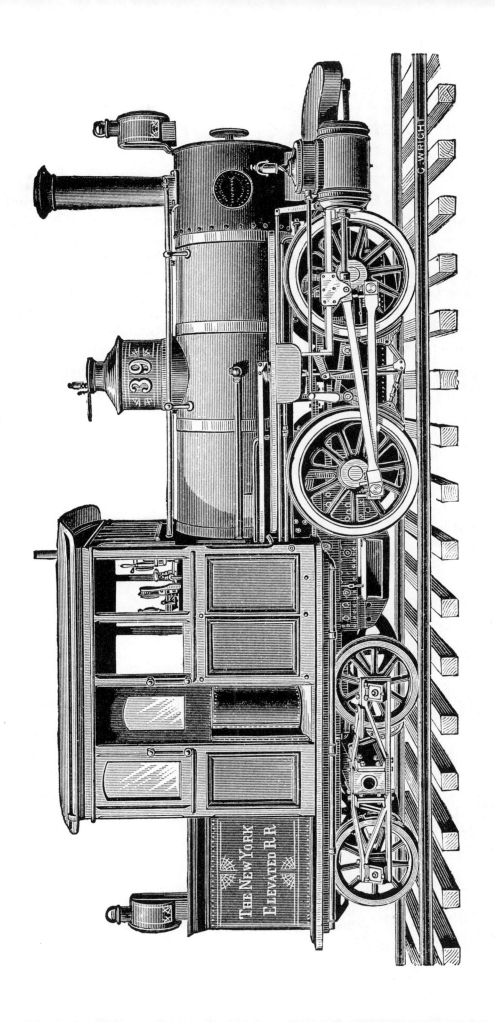

THE *Uncle Dick*, a 2–8–0 tank engine, was designed for service on the temporary switchback laid over the Raton Mountains while the Santa Fe's main line tunnel was being constructed. This temporary line had grades of 316.8 feet per mile and curves of a 359-foot radius, over which this locomotive gave very good service.

The *Uncle Dick* was built by the Baldwin Locomotive Works and had a 1,200-gallon saddle tank on the boiler as well as a separate tender. It could haul a train of nine loaded cars besides its tender up the grade mentioned.

Cylinders 20 by 24 inches   Total weight 115,000 pounds   Drivers 42 inches in diameter   Weight on drivers 100,000 pounds

THIS engine was designed by John E. Wootten of the Philadelphia and Reading Railway for fast passenger service and built at the company's Reading Shops in 1880. It was one of the first to use Wootten's boiler, which was a great improvement over earlier types. This was placed entirely above the drivers, necessitating a higher mounting than usual, but its principal feature was its large grate area designed for burning fine anthracite.

The correct term for any locomotive of this type with the cab mounted as shown (regardless of wheel arrangement) is "Wootten boiler engine." On the Philadelphia & Reading Railway, where they originated, they were called "camelbacks," a nickname generally used on this and many other roads to this day. On the Baltimore & Ohio they were called Mother Hubbards, one reason probably being to differentiate between them and this road's camel engines (Plate 20).

Cylinders 21 by 22 inches   Total weight 96,200 pounds   Drivers 68 inches in diameter   Truck wheels 33 inches in diameter   Weight on drivers 64,250 pounds Total wheelbase 21 feet 1 inch   Rigid wheelbase 6 feet 6 inches

ANOTHER Philadelphia & Reading engine with Wootten's boiler and firebox was this 4–2–2 type built the same year as the 4–4–0. It was also designed for high-speed passenger traffic and intended for use on the two-hour trains over the Bound Brook Line between New York and Philadelphia.

With this wheel arrangement, coupling rods were dispensed with, and to eliminate an excessive load on the drivers a system of equalizing levers was provided. Movable fulcrums controlled by a steam cylinder permitted a greater weight to be applied to the drivers when starting, and when running the excess weight could be transferred to the trailing wheels. This allowed the total weight distribution to be equalized.

This engine was later resold to the Eames Vacuum Brake Company of Boston and it was sent to England to demonstrate this brake system.

Cylinders 18 by 24 inches   Total weight 85,000 pounds   Drivers 78 inches in diameter   Total wheelbase 21 feet 1 inch   Weight on drivers 35,000 to 45,000 pounds   Truck wheel 36 inches in diameter   Trailer wheels 45 inches in diameter

182

THE Pennsylvania Railroad in 1880 designed an improved American or 4–4–0 type of locomotive in order to meet the increasing demands of the fast passenger traffic on its New York Division. This was their Class K (D6, according to reclassification), the first of which was put into service in March, 1881. In all, seventeen of these engines were built up to 1883. They had unusually large driving wheels for that time— 78 inches in diameter. Their appearance, though plain, was extremely symmetrical and a definite improvement over the fancy trimming previously favored. On these engines, probably for the first time, a steam-operated reverse gear was used. This may be seen on the side of the firebox.

With an average train of five cars weighing about 130 tons, the scheduled run between West Philadelphia and Jersey City was 1 hour and 50 minutes for the 88½ miles—an average speed of 48.3 miles an hour.

Cylinders 18 by 24 inches   Total weight 96,700 pounds   Drivers 78 inches in diameter   Weight on drivers 64,900 pounds   Truck wheels 33 inches in diameter   Total wheelbase 22 feet 7½ inches   Rigid wheelbase 7 feet 9 inches

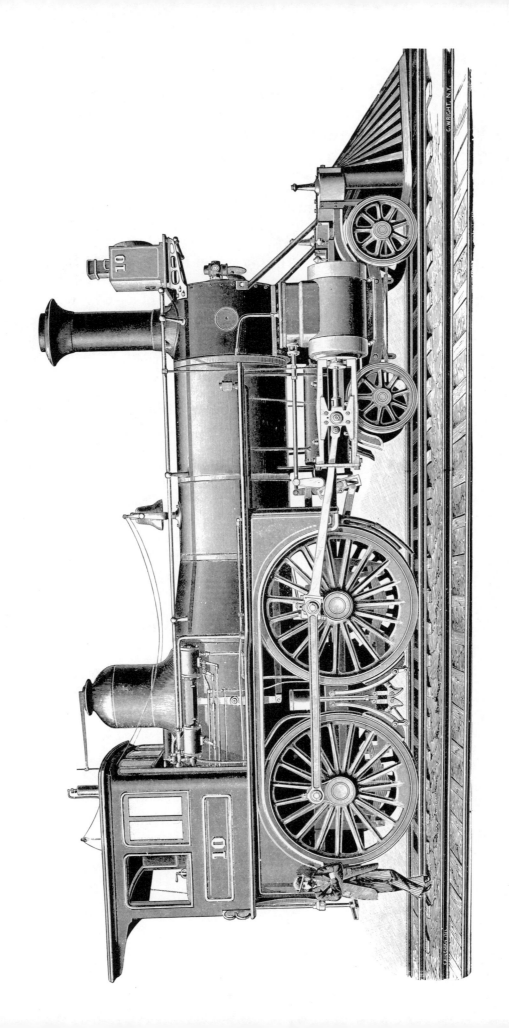

MOST of the locomotives herein mentioned have long since ceased to exist and it is therefore especially interesting to find one of the "old-timers," other than those preserved in museums, which instead of being scrapped was given a new lease on life. This is old Number 2 of the Nevada Central's narrow gauge line which was built by Baldwin in 1881 and now renamed the *Emma Nevada* of the Grizzly Flats Railroad.

The Grizzly Flats Railroad of San Gabriel, California, was founded in December, 1937, when it was heard that the Nevada Central and a portion of the old Carson & Colorado Railroads were to be abandoned. Mr. Ward Kimball and a number of railroad fans, railroad men, model railroaders, and members of the Railway & Locomotive Historical Society quickly decided that some of the historical equipment should be preserved and made the necessary arrangements. On Mr. Kimball's property the first few hundred feet of 35-pound rail were laid early in 1938 in time to receive the locomotive and an old coach from the Carson & Colorado, both having been transported from Nevada on flatcars. The old diamond-stacked Number 2 was found to be intact with its ancient trimmings still in place after sixty years of service. Much hard work has been done by the historically minded railroad fans in restoring both the engine and coach to their original condition so as to make the Grizzly Flats Railroad an authentic replica of early Western railroading.

Cylinders 13 by 18 inches   Total weight 44,000 pounds   Drivers 41 inches in diameter   Weight on drivers 37,000 pounds   Total wheelbase 17 feet 10 inches Rigid wheelbase 12 feet   Fuel coal or wood   Steam pressure 100 pounds

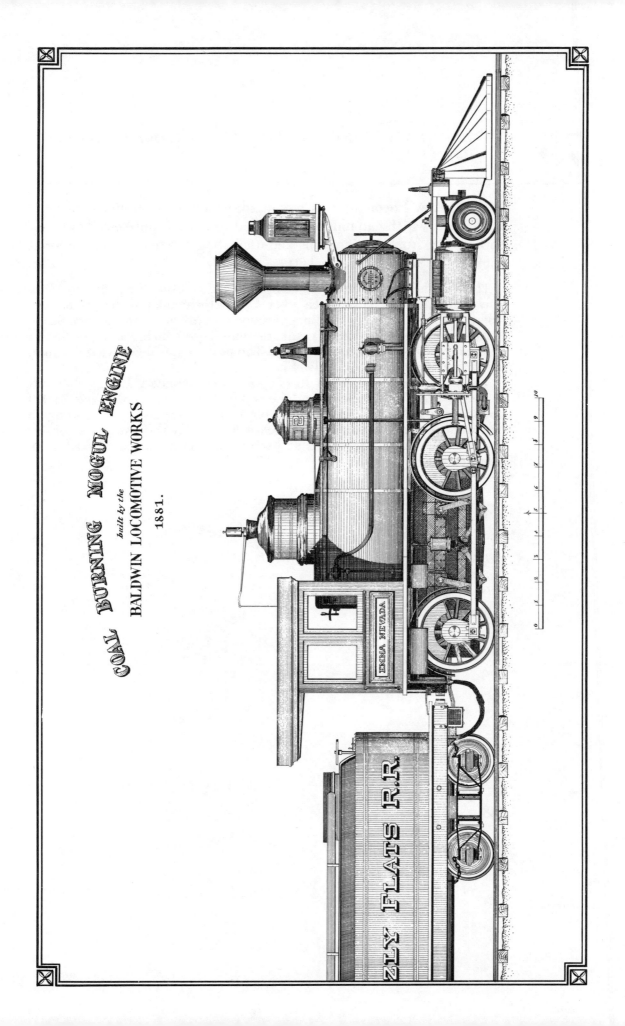

COAL BURNING MOGUL ENGINE

built by the

BALDWIN LOCOMOTIVE WORKS

1881.

75

THE Hinkley Locomotive Works in 1881 built a locomotive called the *H. F. Shaw* which had four cylinders and which was publicized as being entirely free from the pounding and oscillating action of two-cylindered engines. As Sinclair describes it:

The cylinders were arranged side by side, transmitting the power to crank pins diametrically opposite each other. One of the crank pins connected outside the driving wheel at the same position an ordinary crank pin would be located, and carried a double crank, the middle of which was supported in a bearing secured in an outside frame. The bearing was the driving fulcrum, a main rod working at each side of it.

The engine was equivalent to one with two cylinders 16″ by 24″ and driving wheels 63″ in diameter. The weight in working order was 74,000 pounds, of which 25,600 pounds was on the truck wheels. . . . The engine was well designed and built in first-class manner. It was used to a considerable extent on train service in an experimental fashion, and worked quite satisfactorily.

BUILT under the direction of A. J. Stevens, master mechanic of the Central Pacific Railroad, at the Sacramento Shops, this 2–6–2 tank engine was designed for suburban passenger service. Such heavy trains required powerful engines in the morning and evening rush hours for the run between Alameda and Oakland wharf which extended two miles out in the bay, and this class of motive power was the result.

Cylinders 16 by 24 inches   Total wheelbase 28 feet   Driving wheels 50 inches in diameter   Pressure 125 pounds   Rigid wheelbase 14 feet   Truck wheels 26 inches in diameter   Total weight 104,100 pounds   Fuel soft coal, capacity 4 tons   Weight on drivers 80,400 pounds   Water capacity 1,600 gallons

ENGINES with this kind of wheel arrangement became known as the Mastodon type. An experimental one was built in 1856 by Ross Winans and called the *Centipede* but, as a class, this Lehigh Valley locomotive is generally credited with being the first. It was designed by Philip Hofecker, master mechanic of the Beaver Meadow Division, and built at the road's Weatherly Shops.

Cylinders 20 by 26 inches Total weight 101,696 pounds Driving wheels 48 inches in diameter Pressure 125 pounds Weight on drivers 82,432 pounds Truck wheels 24 inches in diameter Total wheelbase 23 feet 2 inches Rigid wheelbase 13 feet ⅜ inches

ANOTHER Mastodon type is this engine built at the Central Pacific's Sacramento Shops to the designs of A. J. Stevens, master mechanic. When finished in 1882, it was the heaviest locomotive in the country.

Two years later the Central Pacific exceeded this effort by building the first 4–10–0 type locomotive, then the most powerful engine in the world. This was the *El Gobernador* and it was generally similar in appearance to the Mastodon except for the additional pair of driving wheels. Its tractive effort was estimated at 34,546 pounds.

Specifications of the locomotive illustrated

Cylinders 19 by 30 inches   Total weight 123,000 pounds   Drivers 54 inches in diameter   Weight on drivers 106,050 pounds   Truck wheels 26 inches in diameter   Total wheelbase 24 feet 11½ inches   Rigid wheelbase 15 feet 9 inches

194

IN 1885 the Pennsylvania Railroad designed and built at its Altoona Shops a new class of Consolidation engine for freight service. It was so successful that a considerable number were built both by the company's shops and the Baldwin Locomotive Works up to the nineties. These were the Class R (new classification H3) locomotives. They are particularly interesting in that they had the first Belpaire boilers to be used on Pennsylvania Railroad motive power.

Cylinders 20 by 24 inches   Total weight 114,620 pounds   Driving wheels 50 inches in diameter   Weight on drivers 100,590 pounds   Total wheelbase 21 feet 9 inches   Rigid wheelbase 13 feet 10 inches   Tractive force 22,850 pounds

The lower section of the illustration shows a cross section of the same locomotive and gives an idea of its various parts. The principles of a steam locomotive's operation are, of course, the same today as always and to the uninitiated perhaps a short résumé of their functions might be interesting .

The illustration does not show the grates or firebox but they are located above the ash pan. The sides as well as the back of the firebox have "water spaces" so that as much heating area as possible is provided. The tubes in the boiler, a few of which are shown, are for the same purpose. Steam is taken from the highest point in the steam dome, being controlled by the throttle valve. From this the steam pipe takes it to the cylinders, the slide valves in the steam chests above them controlling its admission into each end alternatively and thus acting on the piston. The eccentrics shown on the third axle may be set by means of the reverse lever to control the slide valves, both for forward motion or reverse. This method has been superseded by the present external "valve gear" used on more modern engines, but its purpose was the same.

For supplying water to the boiler, the injector is used. This forces water into the boiler by means of a steam jet. A steam cylinder operates the air pump which automatically maintains a fixed pressure in the air reservoir. This supply of compressed air is used for the brake system and all the brakes on the train are simultaneously controlled with the engine brakes. Dry sand kept in the sandbox is applied to the rails if they are slippery or to help adhesion when starting.

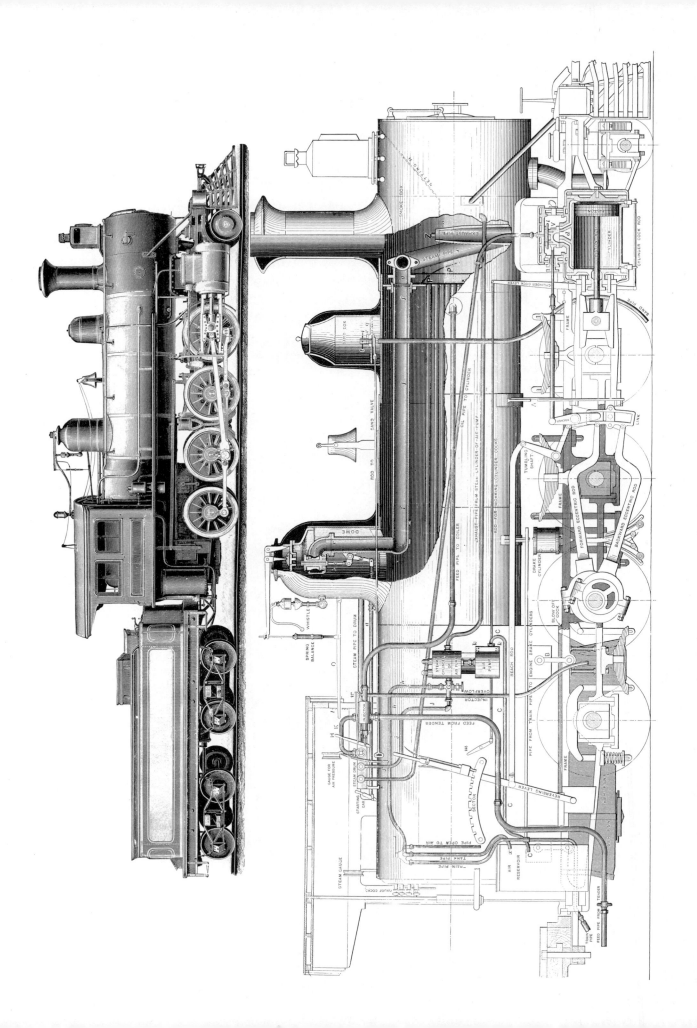

80

THIS American type was one of two engines built for the Lake Shore & Michigan Southern Railroad by the Brooks Locomotive Works at Dunkirk, New York. They were designed by G. W. Stevens, chief of motive power, and used for fast mail trains on the Buffalo and Lake Erie Divisions, which had the heaviest grades as well as being exposed to strong winds from Lake Erie. They carried a much higher steam pressure than was usual for that day—180 pounds.

Cylinders 18 by 24 inches   Weight 110,000 pounds   Driving wheels 69 inches in diameter   On drivers 73,200 pounds   Truck wheels 33 inches in diameter   Total wheelbase 23 feet 11 inches   Rigid wheelbase 9 feet

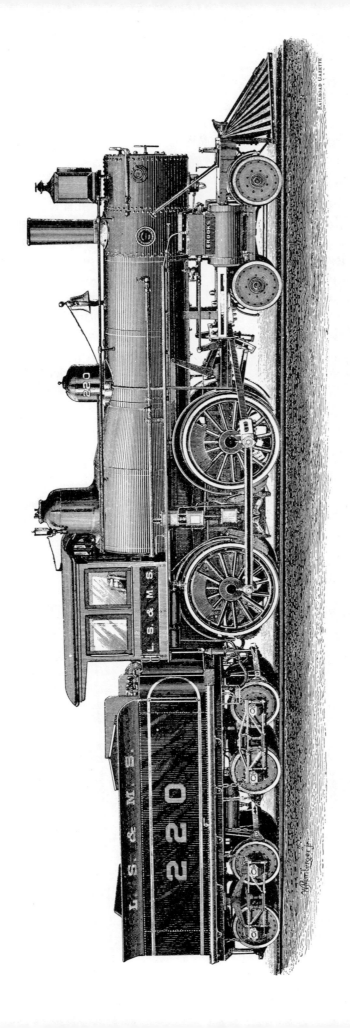

81

HERE is an unusual type of engine to be seen on a Western railroad. Built by the Rogers Locomotive Works to the designs of Clement Hackney, superintendent of motive power of the Union Pacific, they were delivered in 1888. According to contemporary accounts, the severe climate of Nebraska and Wyoming necessitated more protection for the enginemen than would ordinarily be provided on this type of engine and so two cabs were built. The Wootten firebox permitted the use of fine coal or slack taken from the Union Pacific's mines.

Cylinders 18 by 26 inches   Total weight 118,500 pounds   Drivers 63 inches in diameter   Weight on drivers 76,500 pounds   Tractive force 17,965 pounds   Total wheelbase 22 feet 5½ inches   Rigid wheelbase 7 feet 6 inches

THE Pennsylvania Railroad, in grouping its various types of locomotives, had a variety of Class P engines. The oldest were, as reclassified, the D11a of 1883 and the latest, the D14a of 1894. Between these was a type known as the D12a and this is the locomotive illustrated. All the P engines were used in passenger service.

Cylinders 18 by 24 inches   Tractive force 17,000 pounds   Drivers 68 inches in diameter

202

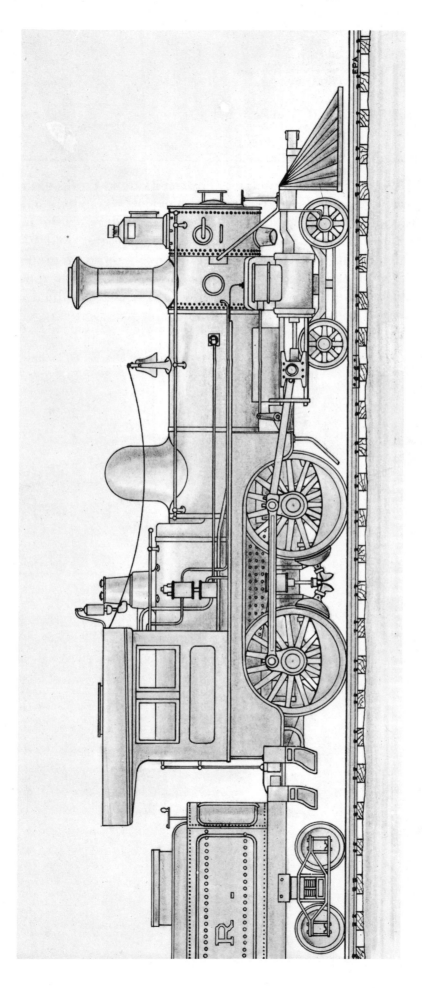

83 *1891. 0–10–0 TANK*

WHEN this engine was delivered by the Baldwin Works to the St. Clair Tunnel Company in 1891, it was the heaviest locomotive in the world. It was designed to haul heavy freight trains through the new tunnel under the St. Clair River between Sarnia, Ontario, and Port Huron, Michigan. This bore was 6,000 feet long with approach grades of 1,950 and 2,500 feet respectively, or an average of 105 feet to the mile. The engine was well designed, all of its weight being available for traction. All wheels with the exception of the center pair were flanged and had brakes. Hard coal was used as fuel.

Cylinders 22 by 28 inches   Weight 195,000 pounds   Drivers 50 inches in diameter Total wheelbase 18 feet 5 inches   Tank capacity 1,800 gallons, 3 tons fuel   Tractive force 58,000 pounds

ST. CLAIR TUNNEL COMPANY

J. H. GEISSEL · DEL.

THE original *Royal Blue* train of the Baltimore & Ohio Railroad was inaugurated in 1889, and in 1890 and 1891 six engines of the M1 class were added to the road's motive power, this being the type assigned to hauling that train.

In 1891 the *Royal Blue* was said to be the fastest train running in America as it covered the distance of 227 miles between New York and Washington in 5 hours at an average speed of 45.5 miles an hour. Three different engines handled the train, the Central Railroad of New Jersey taking it from Jersey City to Bound Brook, a distance of 30 miles in 36 minutes or at an average of 52 miles an hour. From there the Philadelphia & Reading took it the 60 miles to Philadelphia in 73 minutes at the rate of 50 miles an hour. Here one of the M1 engines coupled on for the run to Washington, covering the 137 miles in one minute less than 3 hours (12 minutes being deducted for the ferry crossing from New York).

All three roads over which the train was operated used 4–4–0 engines. The M1 type had 78-inch drivers, the leading pair of which were flangeless.

Cylinders 20 by 24 inches   Weight 116,000 pounds   Weight on drivers 76,000 pounds   Total wheelbase 21 feet 11 inches   Rigid wheelbase 7 feet 6 inches

THE LOCOMOTIVE ENGINEER

THE famous "999" was built at the West Albany Shops of the New York Central & Hudson River Railroad. It made history on May 10, 1893, when it attained the speed of 112.5 miles an hour while pulling the *Empire State Express,* a record which stood for a number of years.

The "999" is still preserved as an example of motive power of the nineties.

Boiler pressure 180 pounds   Drivers 86 inches in diameter

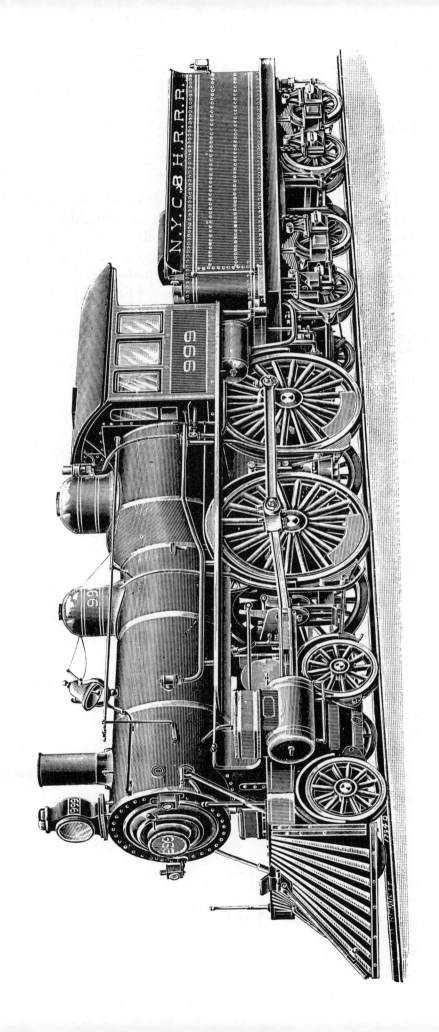

THE Pacific type or 4–6–2 locomotive is usually associated with the first engines of this wheel arrangement built by the Baldwin Works for New Zealand early in the twentieth century. However, some few other locomotives previously had such wheel arrangements, among which were three compound engines built by the Rhode Island Locomotive Works. These were for the Chicago, Milwaukee & St. Paul Railroad in 1893 and designed for fast passenger service.

Cylinders 21 and 31-inch bore by 26-inch stroke (compound)   Drivers 78 inches in diameter   Total weight 143,000 pounds   Total wheelbase 29 feet 9¼ inches   Weight on drivers 88,500 pounds   Rigid wheelbase 13 feet 6 inches   Weight on trailer 18,000 pounds   Weight on truck 36,500 pounds

This illustration and the seven following are from "Transportation Exhibits at the Columbian Exposition." Other than specifications, little information concerning the various locomotives is given.

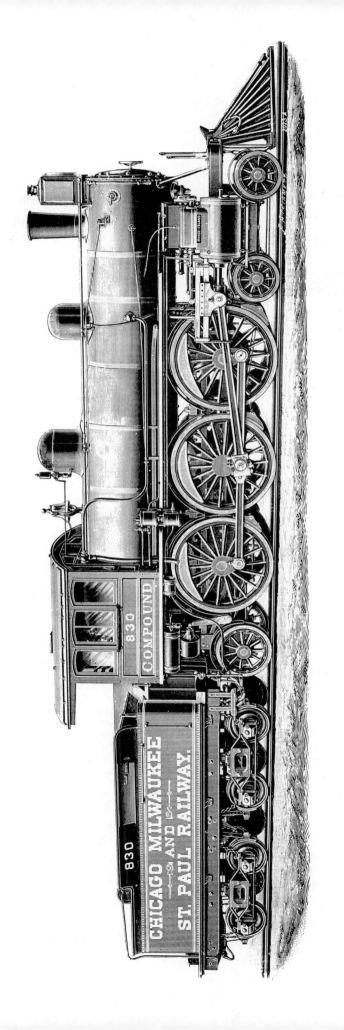

THIS compound 4–4–0 is one of the Rhode Island Locomotive Works engines built for the New York, New Haven & Hartford Railroad. It was designed for passenger service.

Cylinders 21 and 31 inches by 26-inch stroke   Total weight 125,000 pounds Weight on drivers 84,000 pounds   Driving wheels 78 inches in diameter   Total wheelbase 22 feet 9 inches   Rigid wheelbase 19 feet 8 inches

THE Chicago & North Western Railroad obtained this locomotive from the Schenectady Locomotive Works for passenger service. It had driving wheels 69 inches in diameter.

Cylinders 19 by 24 inches   Total weight 129,000 pounds   Weight on drivers 96,000 pounds

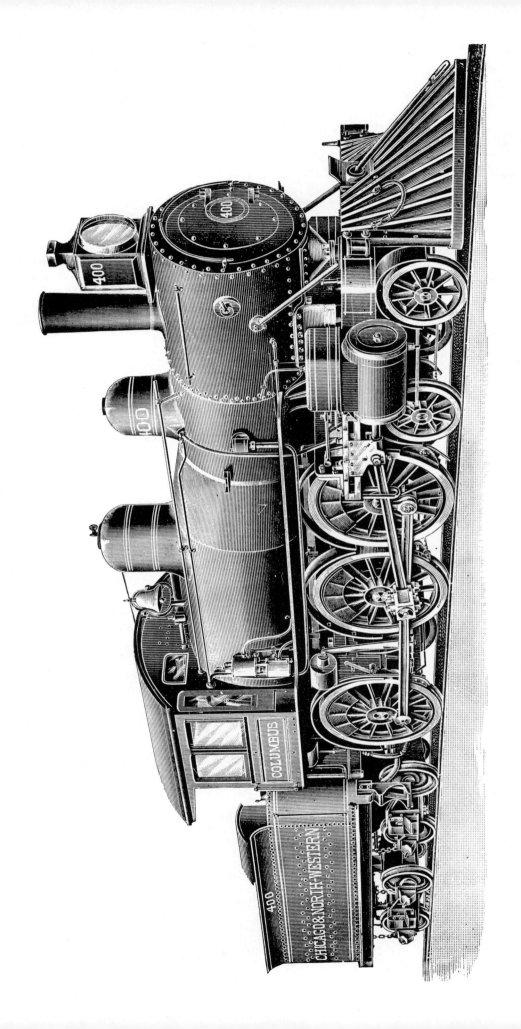

THE Brooks Locomotive Works built this Mogul-type freight engine. It was constructed for the Great Northern Railway. Note that, like Pennsylvania engines, it has the Belpaire boiler.

Cylinders 19 by 24 inches   Total weight 118,000 pounds   Drivers 55 inches in diameter   Weight on drivers 102,000 pounds   Truck wheels 30 inches in diameter   Total wheelbase 21 feet 6 inches   Rigid wheelbase 14 feet

THE heaviest engine in the Baldwin Exhibit at the Columbian Exposition was this Decapod type which was built for the New York, Lake Erie & Western Railroad. It had the Wootten firebox and was a compound engine of the Vauclain type.

Cylinders 16 and 27 inches by 28-inch stroke   Total weight 195,000 pounds Weight on drivers 172,000 pounds   Total wheelbase 27 feet 3 inches   Rigid wheelbase 19 feet 10 inches

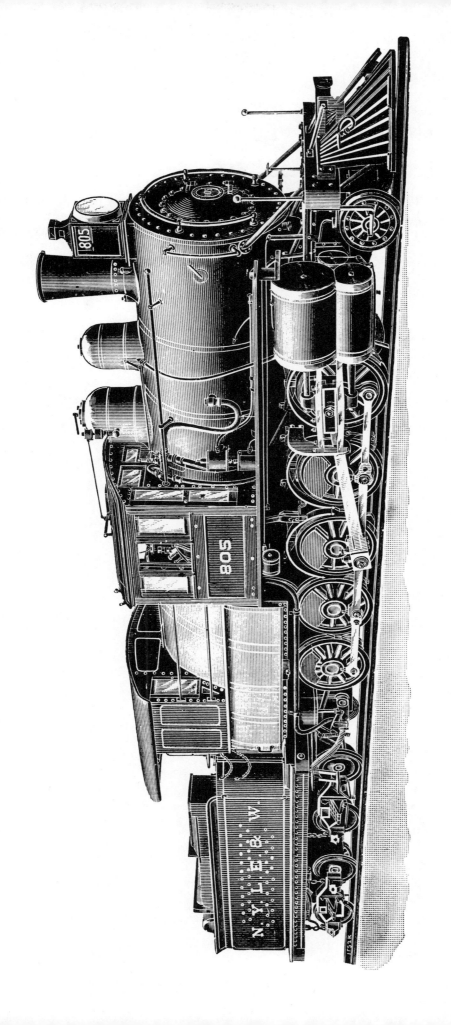

THIS Soo Line Consolidation type was built by the Rhode Island Locomotive Works. It was intended for use in freight service.

Cylinders 21 and 31 inches by 24-inch stroke (compound)   Total weight 130,000 pounds   Weight on drivers 118,200 pounds   Total wheelbase 22 feet 6 inches   Driving wheels 50 inches in diameter   Rigid wheelbase 15 feet

FOR suburban service the Brooks Locomotive Works built this tank engine for the Chicago & Northern Pacific Railroad.

Cylinders 18 by 24 inches   Total weight 166,000 pounds   Weight on drivers 102,000 pounds   Total wheelbase 35 feet 9 inches   Drivers 63 inches in diameter Rigid wheelbase 15 inches   Truck wheels 30 inches in diameter   Water capacity 2,600 gallons   Fuel 4½ tons

THIS Chicago, Burlington & Quincy Railroad 4–4–0 was built by the Rogers Locomotive Works for passenger service. This engine, too, had a Belpaire boiler.

Cylinders 18 by 24 inches   Total weight 102,000 pounds   Fuel soft coal   Weight on drivers 65,000 pounds   Total wheelbase 22 feet 11½ inches   Drivers 69 inches in diameter   Rigid wheelbase 8 feet 6 inches   Truck wheels 37 inches in diameter

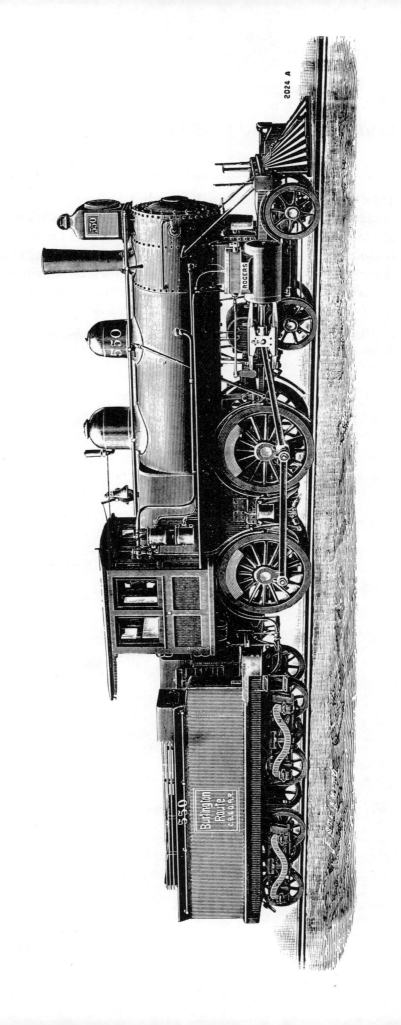

THE first engine to have a Vanderbilt boiler was the ten-wheeler illustrated—the Number 947—which was built at the West Albany Shops of the New York Central & Hudson River Railroad in 1899. This type of boiler used a corrugated, cylindrical firebox which was to effect savings in construction and maintenance costs and which appeared to give satisfactory results—so much so that Baldwin's, a short time later, built several more engines with fireboxes of this design.

Cylinders 19½ by 26 inches   Total weight 160,000 pounds   Drivers 61 inches in diameter   Weight on drivers 113,000 pounds

226

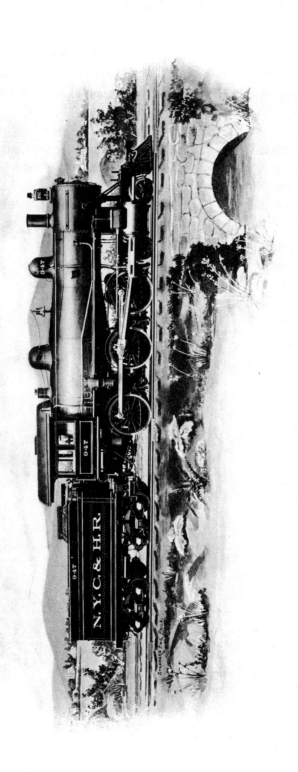

THE first Prairie type or 2–6–2 locomotive was used on the Chicago, Burlington & Quincy Railroad. It was built in 1900 by the Baldwin Locomotive Works. The Prairie is a development from the Mogul or 2–6–0 type, wherein a pair of trailing wheels supports part of the weight of the firebox. It also allows a wider firebox with shorter length permitting easier firing. Prairie type engines have not been built for many years, larger locomotives having taken their place. Most were used in freight service, but some with larger driving wheels were used for passenger traffic.

Cylinders 20 by 24 inches Total weight 168,475 pounds Weight on drivers 129,575 pounds Total wheelbase 28 feet Drivers 64 inches in diameter Rigid wheelbase 12 feet 1 inch Truck wheels 37¼ inches Trailing wheels 37 inches

FIVE more engines with Vanderbilt boilers had been built following the experimental one, all for the New York Central road when the Union Pacific Railway ordered two Consolidation type engines from the Baldwin Locomotive Works. These also had this type of boiler and were delivered in July, 1900, when they were put into freight service.

Cylinders Vauclain compound 15½ and 26 inches by 30-inch stroke   Total weight 196,000 pounds   Weight on drivers 174,000 pounds   Boiler pressure 190 pounds Drivers 57 inches in diameter   Rigid wheelbase 23 feet 11 inches   Rigid wheelbase 15 feet 3 inches

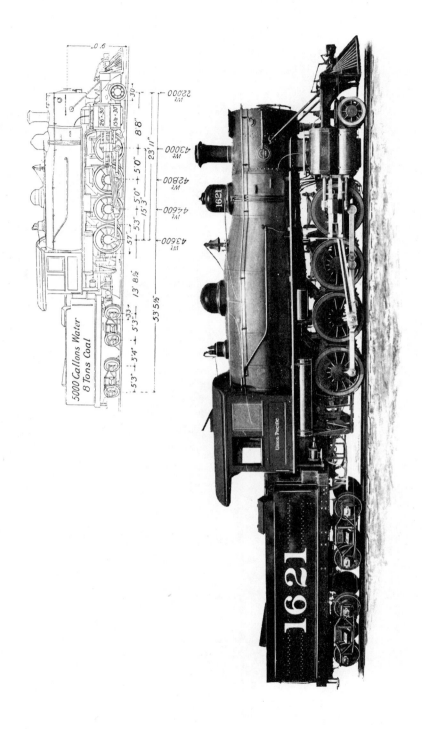

5000 Gallons Water
8 Tons Coal

53' 5½"

13' 8½"

5'-3" 5'-4" 5'-3" 5'-3"

57" 5'-3" 5'-0" 5'-0" 23' 11" 8' 8"

15'-3"

26"–30"

15½"–30"

Wt 43600 Wt 44600 Wt 42800 Wt 43000 Wt 22000

Locomotive Builders
of the United States

Including Location and Approximate Dates in Business

American Locomotive Co.   New York (main plant Schenectady)
    The following combined in 1901 to form this company: 1901–present
        Brooks Locomotive Works
        Cooke Locomotive and Machine Works
        Dickson Manufacturing Company
        Manchester Locomotive Works
        Pittsburgh Locomotive and Car Works
        Rhode Island Locomotive Works (International Power Company)
        Richmond Locomotive Works
        Schenectady Locomotive Works
        Rogers Locomotive Works (Acquired in 1905)

Amoskeag Manufacturing Co.	Manchester, N.H.	1849–1856
J. R. Anderson & Co. (Tredegar Works)	Richmond, Va.	1852–1854
R. A. Anderson Machine Co.	?	1853
Anderson & Delany (Tredegar Works)	Richmond, Va.	1855–1858
Anderson & Souther	Richmond, Va.	1852–1853
Appomattox Locomotive Works	Petersburg, Va.	1856
Aurora Locomotive Works (C. C. Olmstead & Co.)	Aurora, Ind.	1856
M. W. Baldwin (Baldwin Locomotive Works); Baldwin & Vail; Baldwin, Vail & Hufty; Baldwin & Whitney; Baird & Co.; Burnham, Williams	Philadelphia, Pa. (Plant now at Eddystone, Pa.)	1831–present

& Co.; Burnham, Parry Williams & Co., etc.		
Ballardvale Manufacturing Co.	North Andover, Mass.	1848–1849
Baltimore Locomotive Works	Baltimore, Md.	1868
David Bell Co.	Pittsburgh, Pa.	1866–1871
Bemis & Co.	Springfield, Mass.	1857
Blanchard & Kimball	Springfield, Mass.	1854
H. & F. Blandy	Zanesville, O.	1852–1858
H. J. Booth & Co.	San Francisco, Cal.	1861–1868
Boston Locomotive Works (see Hinkley & Drury)		
Seth Boyden	Newark, N.J.	1837–1838
Breese, Kneeland & Co.	Jersey City, N.J.	1852–1857
James Brooks	Philadelphia, Pa.	1836
Brooks Locomotive Works	Dunkirk, N.Y.	1869–1901
Browning, Dunham & Co.	New York, N.Y.	1836–1838
Buffalo Steam Engine Works	Buffalo, N.Y.	1855
D. J. Burr & Co.	Richmond, Va.	1838–1841
Burr & Ettinger	Richmond, Va.	1852
Burr, Pea & Sampson	Richmond, Va.	1846
Campbell, Whittier & Co.	Cambridgeport, Mass.	1866
Chicago Locomotive Works (Scoville)	Chicago, Ill.	1853–1856
Cincinnati Locomotive Works (Moore & Richardson)	Cincinnati, O.	1854–1857
Jabez Coney	South Boston, Mass.	1848
Cooke Locomotive Works	Paterson, N.J.	1882–1901
Cooper, Clark & Co.	Mt. Vernon, O.	1854
Corliss, Nightingale Co.	Providence, R.I.	1851
Stacey Costell	Philadelphia, Pa.	1831
Covington Locomotive Works	Covington, Ky.	1854
Cuyahoga Locomotive Works (Cuyahoga Steam Furnace Co.)	Cleveland, O.	1850–1856
Danforth, Cooke & Co.	Paterson, N.J.	1852–1865
Danforth Locomotive & Machine Co.	Paterson, N.J.	1865–1882
Davenport Locomotive Works	Davenport, Iowa	1897
Davis & Gartner	York, Pa.	1831
Dawson & Bailey	Connellsville, Pa.	1879
Dickson Locomotive Works	Scranton, Pa.	1858–1901
Denmead & Son	Baltimore, Md.	1852–1859
Detroit Locomotive Works	Detroit, Mich.	1854–1867
D. H. Dotterer & Co.	Reading, Pa.	1839–1842
Thomas Dotterer	Charleston, S.C.	1837
Dunbar & Co.	New York, N.Y.	1836
H. R. Dunham & Co.	New York, N.Y.	1836–1838
Eason & Dotterer	Charleston, S.C.	1833–1838
Eastwick & Harrison	Philadelphia, Pa.	1839–1842

234

Essex Co.	Lawrence, Mass.	1850–1852
Galion Locomotive Works	Galion, O.	1856
Garrett & Eastwick	Philadelphia, Pa.	1836–1838
Globe Locomotive Works (see John Souther)		
Grant Locomotive Works	Paterson, N.J. & Chicago, Ill.	1863–1883
A. Harkness	Cincinnati, O.	1846–1848
A. Harkness & Son	Cincinnati, O.	1848–1852
Harkness & Co.	Cincinnati, O.	1847–1849
Harkness & Sons	Cincinnati, O.	1851–1854
Harkness, Moore & Co.	Cincinnati, O.	1852–1853
Heyward & Bartlett	Baltimore, Md.	1864–1873
Hinkley & Drury, Hinkley & Williams Hinkley Locomotive Works	Boston, Mass.	1841–1889
W. T. James	New York, N.Y.	1831
Jersey City Locomotive Works	Jersey City, N.J.	1858–1863
Kirk	Cambridgeport, Mass.	1850–1852
Lewis Kirk	Reading, Pa.	–1858
Lancaster Locomotive Works	Lancaster, Pa.	1855–1861
A. Latham & Co.	White River Junction, Vt.	1854–1856
Lawrence Machine Shop	Lawrence, Mass.	1852–1857
Lima Locomotive Works	Lima, O.	1879–present
Locks & Canals Co. (Proprietors of Locks and Canals on the Merrimac River)	Lowell, Mass.	1835–1844
Long & Norris	Philadelphia, Pa.	1833
Louisville Locomotive Works	Louisville, Ky.	1871
Lowell Machine Shops	Lowell, Mass.	1845–1854
McClurg, Wade & Co.	Pittsburgh, Pa.	1834–1837
McKay & Aldus Iron Works	East Boston, Mass.	1864–1868
J. McLeish	Charleston, S.C.	1851
McLeish & Smith	Charleston, S.C.	1837
Walter McQueen	Albany, N.Y.	1840
Manchester Locomotive Works	Manchester, N.H.	1856–1901
William Mason (Mason Machine Works)	Taunton, Mass.	1853–1890
Matfield Manufacturing Co.	East Bridgewater, Mass.	1854–1857
Matteawan Machine Co.	Fishkill Landing, N.Y. (Beacon)	1849
Menominee Locomotive Works (Lee & Walton)	Milwaukee, Wis.	1852–1857
Mill Dam Foundry	Boston, Mass.	1834–1835
E. L. Miller	Charleston, S.C.	1833–1834
Moore & Richardson (see Cincinnati Locomotive Works)		
Mount Savage Locomotive Works	Mt. Savage, Md.	1875–1885

Murray & Hazelhurst	Baltimore, Md.	1854–1857
Nashville Manufacturing Co.	Nashville, Tenn.	1852–1853
National Locomotive Works	Connellsville, Pa.	1890–1895
New Castle Manufacturing Co.	New Castle, Del.	1831–1857
New Jersey Locomotive and Machine Co.	Paterson, N.J.	1845–1863
New York Locomotive Works (see Breese, Kneeland & Co.)	Jersey City, N.J.	1852–1857
New York Locomotive Works	Rome, N.Y.	1880–1895
Niles & Co.	Cincinnati, O.	1852–1859
R. Norris & Son	Philadelphia, Pa.	1853–1868
E. S. Norris	Schenectady, N.Y.	1849–1849
E. S. Norris	Lancaster, Pa. & Schenectady, N.Y.	1864–1867
William Norris	Philadelphia, Pa.	1835–1853
Palm & Robertson	St. Louis, Mo.	1853–1858
Pittsburgh Locomotive Works	Pittsburgh, Pa.	1867–1901
H. K. Porter Co.	Pittsburgh, Pa.	1866–present
Portland Locomotive Works	Portland, Me.	1848–1907
Poughkeepsie Locomotive Works	Poughkeepsie, N.Y.	1838
Rhode Island Locomotive Works	Providence, R.I.	1866–1901
Richmond Locomotive Works	Richmond, Va.	1886–1901
Rogers, Ketchum & Grosvenor	Paterson, N.J.	1837–1856
Rogers Locomotive & Machine Works; & Rogers Locomotive Works	Paterson, N.J.	1856–1901
Schenectady Locomotive Works	Schenectady, N.Y.	1851–1901
Coleman Sellers & Son	Philadelphia, Pa.	1836–1841
Smith & Perkins	Alexandria, Va.	1851–1857
R. C. & T. Smith	Alexandria, Va.	1851
T. W. Smith	Alexandria, Va.	1837
John Souther (Globe Works)	South Boston, Mass.	1848–1864
Springfield Car & Engine Co.	Springfield, Mass.	1848–1851
William Swinburne	Paterson, N.J.	1851–1857
Swinburne, Smith & Co.	Paterson, N.J.	1845–1857
Talbott & Bros.	Richmond, Va.	1849–1852
Taunton Locomotive Works	Taunton, Mass.	1847–1889
Tredegar Works	Richmond, Va.	1850–186-
Trenton Locomotive Works	Trenton, N.J.	1853–1857
Virginia Locomotive & Car Manufacturing Co.	Alexandria, Va.	1856
Vulcan Iron Works	Wilkes-Barre, Pa.	1848–present
Vulcan Iron Works	San Francisco, Cal.	1862
Uriah Wells	Petersburg, Va.	1851–1857
West Point Foundry	New York, N.Y.	1830–1835
Seth Wilmarth	Boston, Mass.	1848–1855
Ross Winans	Baltimore, Md.	1837–1860

Other locomotive builders which may be added to the above list, though some may be identified with certain of the firms above mentioned, are:

Cold Spring Foundry	Matteawan, N.Y.	184–
George Coney & Co.	Ballardvale, Mass.	
De Graff & Kendrick	Detroit, Mich.	
Dennis, Wood & Russell	Auburn, N.Y.	
A. L. Greer & Co.	Covington, Ky.	
Kentucky Locomotive Works	Louisville, Ky.	
McKay Iron and Locomotive Co.	Jersey City, N.J.	1869
H. H. Scoville & Sons	Chicago, Ill.	
E. Thrasher & Co.	Dayton, O.	
White River Junction Iron Works	White River Junction, Vt.	

(Due to meager information regarding many little-known shops, this list makes no pretense of being complete or entirely accurate. Most of the builders that at one time or another were in existence are, however, included.)

Whyte's System of Locomotive Classification

(about 1900)

040		4 WHEEL
060		6 WHEEL
0440		ARTICULATED
0660		ARTICULATED
2440		ARTICULATED
080		8 WHEEL
240		4 COUPLED
260		MOGUL
280		CONSOLIDATION
2100		DECAPOD
440		8 WHEEL
460		10 "
480		12 "
042		4 COUPLED & TRAILING
062		6 " " "
082		8 " " "
044		FORNEY 4 COUPLED
064		FORNEY 6 COUPLED
046		" 4 "
066		" 6 "
242		COLUMBIA
262		PRAIRIE
282		MIKADO
2102		10 COUPLED
244		4 "
264		6 "
284		8 "
246		4 "
266		6 "
442		ATLANTIC
462		PACIFIC
444		4 COUPLED DOUBLE ENDER
464		6 " " "
446		4 " " "

238

Bibliography

Bell, Snowden. *Early Motive Power on the Baltimore & Ohio Railroad.* New York: Angus Sinclair Co., 1912.

Cooley, Thomas M., ed. *The American Railway.* New York: Charles Scribners' Sons, 1889.

Dredge, James. *Transportation Exhibits at the Columbian Exposition.* New York: John Wiley & Sons, 1894.

Dunbar, Seymour. *A History of Travel in America.* Indianapolis: The Bobbs-Merrill Co., 1915.

Earle, Thomas. *A Treatise on Rail-Roads and Internal Communications.* Philadelphia: John Grigg, 1830.

Harrison, Joseph, Jr. *The Locomotive Engine.* Philadelphia: George Gebbie, 1872.

History of the Baldwin Locomotive Works. Philadelphia: Baldwin Locomotive Works, 1924.

Mott, Edward Harold. *Between the Ocean and the Lakes, The Story of Erie.* New York: John S. Collins, 1901.

Railroad Gazette, issue for 1882.

Railway & Locomotive Engineering, issues for 1889–1925.

Recent Locomotives. Reprint from *Railroad Gazette,* 1883.

Record of Recent Construction. Nos. 21 to 30. Philadelphia: Baldwin Locomotive Works, 1901.

Sinclair, Angus. *Development of the Locomotive Engine.* New York: Angus Sinclair Co., 1907.

Sipes, William B. *The Pennsylvania Railroad, Historical & Descriptive.* Philadelphia: Pennsylvania Railroad, 1875.

Warner, Paul T. *Motive Power Development on the Pennsylvania Railroad.* Philadelphia: Baldwin Locomotive Works, 1924.